This Book Belongs To:

_____

❧

C·Z·GUEST'S
5 SEASONS OF
GARDENING

C·Z· GUEST'S 5 SEASONS OF GARDENING

C·Z· GUEST

Photographs by Elvin McDonald

A BULFINCH PRESS BOOK

Little, Brown and Company • Boston • Toronto • London

First Edition

Library of Congress Cataloging-in-Publication Data
Guest, C. Z.
        C. Z. Guest's 5 seasons of gardening/
C. Z. Guest; photographs by Elvin McDonald.
—1st ed.
        p.   cm.
        "A Bulfinch Press book."
        Includes index.
        ISBN 0-8212-1897-2
        1. Gardening.   I. McDonald, Elvin.   II. Title.
        III. Title: C. Z. Guest's five seasons of
gardening.   IV. Title: 5 seasons of gardening.
        SB453.G875   1992
        635.9'53—dc20   91-42311

Bulfinch Press is an imprint and trademark of Little, Brown and Company (Inc.)
Published simultaneously in Canada by Little, Brown & Company (Canada) Limited

PRINTED IN SINGAPORE

CONTENTS

This lovely cameo shows my mother, my two sisters, my brother, and me in the late 1930s.
Our family property had a big pool and fountain with pond lilies and goldfish. I realize now that they were
the hardy types of water lilies that come back year after year with no particular care. Blue skies, puffy white clouds,
and pond lilies where bullfrogs sunned themselves—what more could a child want!

C·Z·GUEST'S 5 SEASONS OF GARDENING

Introduction

Flowers are so much a part of my life—every day of the year. They add mood, fragrance, and color to every room in my house. Without flowers, I'd find life very dismal.

My love for flowers started in my mother's garden and greenhouses at our family property on the North Shore of Boston, where I grew up. Although my mother wasn't really a gardener herself, she loved flowers with a passion, and wherever we went, my earliest memories are of carloads of flowers accompanying us. Our property on the North Shore had three gardens: two extensive formal gardens, which included beds of roses, lilies, all varieties of annuals and perennials, and a big pool and fountain with pond lilies and goldfish; plus a huge kitchen garden, which supplied the house with multitudes of edibles. The kitchen garden also provided every size, shape, and color of cut flowers that one could imagine, including zinnias, cosmos, peonies, dahlias, lilies, marigolds, chrysanthemums, asters, nasturtiums, strawflowers, poppies, snapdragons, sunflowers, salvias, lobelias, larkspurs, foxgloves, gaillardias, delphiniums, sweet Williams, sweet peas, and corn flowers—those are just the ones I can remember! When I wasn't romping around the grounds on my black pony, Jack, I was following at the heels of my favorite pal, Mr. Buffett, my mother's head gardener.

William Buffett was in his forties when I was a child. He had been with the family for years, much longer than I had; and he was there after I left. I used to marvel at his knowledge of flowers, the way his gentle hands could swiftly but delicately handle little seedlings, how he repotted plants, how he lovingly cut flowers. He was almost like a surgeon. He lived with flowers, and he loved his work. He had a knack for making his work fun and for educating a young child to feel the same love for flowers that he felt.

There were two things Mr. Buffett preached on a regular basis. One I learned well, and the second I am still learning. First, Mr. Buffett was one of the most organized people I have ever known. He was at work by seven every morning, and he always had a plan for the day. He knew where he was going, what he was going to do, and what the people he supervised were going to do. I remember him each evening meeting with the other gardeners to discuss their plan for the next day. I now realize that he had developed a way to make things work efficiently: a system. Having a system is the only way to have a successful garden. You must make notes of your triumphs and your failures as Mr. Buffett did so that you know how to repeat your successes and how not to make the same mistakes again.

Second, you've heard the saying that *patience* is a

virtue. Well, it's a virtue that I've never had. I believe that lack of patience comes from being energetic and interested; it's so hard for a young child to wait. But patience is one thing that you will learn from having a garden. You can't hurry Mother Nature. I remember constantly asking Mr. Buffett, "Can't I look now?" or "Are they ready yet?" Mr. Buffett's standard answer: "In a week or two." (Mr. Buffett was probably not completely aware of the impression he was making on this little blond imp who so faithfully dogged his footsteps, but the seeds that he planted in my brain have guided me throughout my life.)

After I married my late husband, Winston, I was able to create and develop my own gardens at our houses on Long Island, in Palm Beach, and in Virginia. My main residence is Templeton, in Old Westbury, Long Island, New York, and that is where my most complex gardens and greenhouses are situated. I have a formal rose garden enclosed by a brick wall just off the terrace; then, extending from a main wall of the house, more roses and hardy perennial flowers mixed together in two beds, these on either side of five topiary trees; and from here, the grassy path leads into the kitchen garden. I have many different varieties of roses: Peace, Tropicana, Queen Elizabeth, J.F.K., Chicago Peace, Garden Party, Oregold, Mojave, Hawaii, Tanya, King's Ransom, Ginger, and Helen Traubel, to name a few.

The kitchen garden is really my pride and joy. I can spend hours there digging, planting, picking, snipping, looking, inspecting, nibbling, and just plain relaxing. The kitchen garden consists of beds of my favorite vegetables (string beans, peas, carrots, beets, radishes, lettuce, broccoli, peppers, cucumbers, squash, pumpkins, onions, chard, tomatoes, eggplants, corn, and potatoes), an herb bed (mint, tarragon, basil, parsley, chives, dill, rosemary, oregano, and thyme), a patch for horseradish, alpine strawberry borders, beds for annuals (zinnias, marigolds, asters, sweet Williams,

candytufts, nasturtiums, pansies, strawflowers), beds of perennials (hardy chrysanthemums, peonies, lilies, columbine, Shasta daisies, oriental poppies, Japanese and Siberian irises, primroses, hollyhocks), and special test beds for seeds sent to me by various seed companies to test their durability, vigor, and disease resistance in my area. I have a staff of several gardeners to help me keep all this going.

The kitchen garden is really like a little factory that produces abundantly for the whole household. We all take pride in the wonderful vegetables and beautiful flowers this garden gives us. Of course, I can't cook at all, but I love fabulous food that's beautifully prepared. Thanks to my multitalented staff, all of whom have been with me forever (Roger Houssaye, the incomparable French chef; Jan Bigilia, my personal maid turned summertime chef and gardener; Mademoiselle Marie Mannoni, our governess, who now takes care of my every need; and Mary Pascucci, gardener and flower expert), the fruits of our kitchen garden are turned into legendary dinners. As Truman Capote once said, "Vegetables, vegetables, vegetables! At Babe Paley's table, or Bunny Mellon's or Betsy Whitney's or Ceezie's —haven't you noticed how extraordinary the vegetables are? The smallest, most succulent peas, lettuce, the most delicate baby corn, asparagus, limas the size of cuticles, the tiny sweet radishes, everything so fresh, almost unborn—that's what you can do when you have an acre or so of gardens."

Just off the kitchen garden are my two greenhouses; the larger one is for orchids and potted plants, and the smaller one is a growing house. My interest in orchids was started by my mother. After I was married, she sent me an orchid plant each year for my birthday, my wedding anniversary, and Christmas. Before long, I had quite an extensive collection, and as this collection grew, so did my interest and knowledge. Orchids are truly the most intriguing and exotic of all flowers. They are seductive yet mysterious. The beauty of some cannot be fully appreciated by the naked eye. The center of a tiny renanthera orchid, when inspected under a magnifying glass, reveals a dazzling meld of shades of rose, red, and pink, while a zygopetalum shows an unusual blend of greens and blues. Some orchids have a fragrance only during the night, some only during the day. Some species dare to bloom only one day of the year.

In my greenhouse, I have sometimes as many as fifteen species of orchids: vanda, paphiopedilum, dendrobium, miltonia, oncidium, epidendrum, zygopetalum, schomburgkia, rhyncostylus, laeliocattleya, cattleya, miniature cymbidium, phalaenopsis, phaius, and ascocentrum. I prefer the orchids that stay in bloom for several weeks. When they are in full bloom, they are brought into the house, where they make a perfect houseplant. I love to have a room filled with many colors and kinds of flowers. I also do something that very few people would ever dream of doing. I mix orchids with other flowers. Often, I'll put an orchid plant next to a lovely arrangement of roses and peonies. Oddly enough, all flowers, no matter what size, color, or shape, seem to complement one another.

In the greenhouse, I expect all of my plants to get along! In addition to orchids, I have benches of potted plants such as geranium, hibiscus, clivia, sweet olive, amaryllis, lantana, nasturtium, azalea, jasmine, camellia, stephanotis, and some miniature fruit trees: lemon, orange, and lime. These are all in the same greenhouse but in different sections with different temperature controls.

I always plan my garden around what I like to call the five seasons of the year. I think of these as winter, spring, summer, fall, and the holidays. I like to plan the holidays as a fifth season because it's so much fun to have fragrant flowers in festive colors throughout the house on Halloween, Thanksgiving, Christmas, and New Year's. For Halloween and Thanksgiving, the colors that I like are mostly yellow and orange. For Christmas and New Year's: white and red. The whole year with my gardens is planned very carefully to give my house a feeling of joy and pleasure all through the seasons.

I want my book, *5 Seasons of Gardening,* to tell you exactly how I like to garden, what I do with my plants, what kinds of flowers I like and how I like to arrange them, what I think about gardening, and how I organize. Through the lovely photographs in this book, I hope to share with you some of my own unique ideas about how a garden should look and how flowers should be used in arrangements and decorations. I may do things differently than you would expect, but that's my style, and it works beautifully for me.

If this book can give you some new ideas and help you with your garden life, then I'll be happy. You may want to do some things exactly as I do or you may modify my ideas to suit your own taste, but that's what learning is all about. The most important thing about gardening is to enjoy yourself and have a good time. I've always felt that having a garden is like having a good and loyal friend. All the love and tender care you put into it will be returned. After reading this book, I hope you have the same pleasure and fulfillment from your garden as I have from mine.

Dainty Bess rose.

Hybrid geraniums from seeds are displayed on the mantel of my small dining room. With its dark burgundy walls and hunting prints, it is one of the coziest places I have in the winter.

$\mathcal{1}$ Winter

Winter is the quiet time to start thinking about and preparing for your garden.

Plan Ahead

To have a good garden, you must organize well, and winter is the time to do just that. If you wait until spring, you will be too busy, and it will be too late. Start by making notes of what you want your garden to be *season by season* for the whole year. With gardening, you must always plan ahead.

When you're sitting by the fire looking out at the winter scenery, surround yourself with as many garden catalogs as possible. My two favorites are *Wayside Gardens* and *Burpee Gardens.* Leaf through the catalogs, look at the pretty pictures, and decide what kinds of flowers and vegetables you like.

It's a good idea to have your season-by-season plan prepared by the end of December. Write down in your garden planner the flowers and vegetables of your choice, when to plant, their growing needs, height, when they bloom or produce vegetables, and for how long. This is a big job that takes a lot of careful consideration; but, once you've completed your schedule, you're on your way to being well organized.

SOME CONSIDERATIONS WHEN CHOOSING FLOWERS

First, choose what type of garden you want. A kitchen garden supplies the house with edibles and flowers.

If you're not interested in growing vegetables, you can have just a cutting garden to fill your house with beautiful bouquets. If you decide on a cutting garden, consider the color schemes in your house. In which rooms do you want flowers and what shades will complement the colors of each room? In my blue-and-white salon, just off my front foyer, I use white and blue flowers year round. And in my dining room, which is predominantly green, with a woodsy feeling, I decorate with flowers and plants in every color and shape. I find everything in nature goes with green.

Perhaps you want a formal garden; then, colors and shapes are the most important considerations. Formality in a garden needn't be off-putting; in fact, I think it is more easily achieved than a casual approach. Formality is based on balance, with a symmetrical arrangement of beds and plantings. There is something about the simplicity of a formal garden that always makes me feel at home right away.

Second, always keep in mind which flowers will thrive in your area. The growing zones for each flower are clearly defined in the catalogs. Also, consider their needs—full sun or partial shade, acidic or alkaline soil (most flowers will thrive in soil with a pH range from 5.5 to 6.8, which is moderately to slightly acidic). And consider whether they are annuals or perennials.

Third, pay attention to blooming times, so that all your flowers will not bloom in summer and none in the spring and fall—unless your garden is at a summer house, and this is the only season you care about.

Last, determine the heights of your flower choices and the general shapes of the plants—tall and slender, such as hollyhocks, or low and spreading, such as sweet alyssum.

WHAT ABOUT VEGETABLES?

It is not necessary to have a separate garden for veggies. As a matter of fact, some vegetables and flowers make good "bedmates." Scientists can't explain it, but experi-enced gardeners have found that certain plantings combining vegetables and flowers, vegetables with herbs, or even vegetables with vegetables actually enhance growth and reduce insect and disease troubles. Keep this in mind when ordering seeds. Also, remem-ber that some companion plantings may work well for one gardener but not for another—weather, soil, insect populations, and other factors all contribute to success or failure. Here are some worth trying:

FAR LEFT: *Cultivate a cutting garden so you can fill your house with beautiful bouquets. I especially enjoy little bouquets made from a variety of old-fashioned flowers and herbs such as these of nasturtiums and pansies; yellow snapdragons and golden sage; cattleya orchid and Gloriosa daisy; red dianthus, white achillea, and blue daisy; and purple-veined lavender miniature hollyhock with frilly purple perilla.*

LEFT: *Always consider the height and general shape of your flower choices. Hollyhocks such as these in my kitchen garden grow to six feet—and more!*

ABOVE: *Sweet alyssum carpets the ground with white, pink, or purple. Shear it back after a wave of bloom, and it will soon be covered with fresh flowers.*

Swiss chard and rhubarb chard make compatible and attractive bedmates for asparagus, especially when the latter has its red berries, in autumn.

Asparagus: compatible with chard, tomatoes, basil, or parsley

Beans: compatible with marigolds, celery, or potatoes

Beets: compatible with carrots, onions, or members of the brassica family (kohlrabi, cauliflower, kale, broccoli, Brussels sprouts, turnips, cabbage)

Carrots: compatible with onions or sage (which repel carrot fly), beets, or peas

Cucumbers: compatible with corn or radishes (to repel cucumber beetles)

Lettuce: compatible with cabbage, onions, or radishes

Marigolds: compatible anywhere (and are said to cut nematode populations)

Nasturtiums: compatible with potatoes or squash

Onions: compatible with carrots, lettuce, or radishes

Peas: compatible with beans, carrots, corn, potatoes, or turnips

Peppers: compatible with carrots, eggplants, onions, or tomatoes

Potatoes: compatible with corn, eggplants, or peas

Radishes: compatible with carrots or lettuce

Squash: compatible with beans, corn, or radishes

Strawberries: compatible with borage, lettuce, or spinach

Tomatoes: compatible with carrots, mint, spinach, lettuce, basil, or nasturtiums

Turnips: compatible with peas

Other combinations can be disastrous. Some species are incompatible and simply cannot get along; some attract the same disease and insect pests; and some are said to inhibit the growth of others.

Asparagus: incompatible with onions or garlic

Beans: incompatible with onions, garlic, shallots, or gladiolus

Beets: incompatible with pole beans

Cabbages and kohlrabies: incompatible with tomatoes or strawberries

Carrots: incompatible with dill

Corn: incompatible with tomatoes (both are susceptible to corn earworm)

Cucumbers: incompatible with potatoes or sage

Onions: incompatible with peas or beans

Peas: incompatible with shallots, onions, or garlic

Potatoes: incompatible with tomatoes or sunflowers

Tomatoes: incompatible with fennel, corn, or kohlrabi

Fennel, sunflowers, and walnut trees (with growth inhibitors): incompatible with most other species.

As you lay out your garden plan, consider interplanting as well as which vegetables are compatible neighbors. A good example is interplanting corn with pumpkins. To be effective, it is a good idea to sow the pumpkin seed as early as possible (or even start indoors) and plant the corn several weeks later. If the corn gets big too fast, it will shade the pumpkin vines as they begin to flower and trap heat, thus raising already high summer temperatures even more; honeybees are generally active pollinating between 70 and 90 degrees F (20 to 34 degrees C), and if temperatures go much higher, the bees simply will not perform. Because pollination is also the key to corn production, it is best to plant corn in blocks of at least three or four rows, even when interplanting. If this is not possible, or if the weather is simply too hot, you can try hand pollination. When the tassels are shedding pollen, simply shake them onto the silks. Without adequate pollination, ears of corn will not fill out completely.

When planning your garden, you also need to keep timing in mind—which vegetables and flowers are hardy and can withstand cool temperatures and which are more tender and require warmer weather to thrive. Here is a list, in sequence, of some vegetables to plant in spring.

The hardiest kinds are lettuces and salad greens, cabbages, radishes, most edible-pod and garden peas, spinach, leeks, hardy onion varieties, and garlic, to name a few. I begin planting these in early spring—April on Long Island.

By mid spring, late April, or early May in my area,

I plant half-hardy, cool-season crops such as carrots, potatoes, Swiss chard, cauliflower, endive, and celery.

When the temperature at night is at least 60 degrees F (15 degrees C), warm-season, tender vegetables such as lima beans, sweet corn, snap beans, New Zealand spinach, and soybeans can survive outdoors.

Other very tender, warm-season crops are eggplants, tomatoes, peppers, pumpkins, squash, cucumbers, and watermelons. I start tomatoes, peppers, eggplants, and all the very long-season crops indoors in late winter to give them a head start in our relatively short Long Island growing season.

Annual flowers, such as cosmos, nasturtiums, marigolds, sunflowers, zinnias, strawflowers, and calendulas, are always considered warm-season plants because their seeds simply won't germinate before the weather warms, and the first frost in fall marks the end of their season. Perennials, on the other hand, are hardy and can be planted early, and they stay in the ground year round.

LEFT: *Marigolds are compatible anywhere. In the foreground on a tepee is a blue clematis. Beyond are rows of green oak-leaf lettuce, green beans, leeks, eggplants, and two big beds of roses and dahlias for cutting.*

RIGHT: *Remember, tomatoes are incompatible with fennel, corn, or kohlrabi; in other words, don't ask it to be a bedmate to any of the others!*

LEFT: *A vibrant bunch of cut strawflowers glow in the morning sun.*

RIGHT: *Sensation cosmos, which come also in pale pink and pure white, are irresistible to the bees. I like to cut a whole bunch so they fill a small jar or vase with their sparkling, fresh colors.*

Getting Started

Once you've decided what flowers and vegetables you are going to grow in your garden, it is best to order quickly the desired seeds through the catalog. I stress how important it is to act early because many of the seed companies offer discounts to those who order by January or the beginning of February. It pays to be an early bird!

After the seeds arrive, you may start your vegetables and flowers in flats in the greenhouse or wait until spring to sow outdoors.

HINTS FOR ORDERING SEEDS FROM CATALOGS

Today, very few mail-order seed companies grow their own seed, and most of those that do are specialists in a particular category, such as vegetables. In fact, almost

*Drought- and heat-tolerant annual
flowers such as Sun Red zinnias keep the
garden colorful and provide the makings
for bouquets even when the weather
turns unseasonably hot and dry. Adding
an organic mulch around the plants will
make the most of available moisture.*

RIGHT: *Sombrero zinnia is an example of
a flower that can be dried in an upright
position on a wire-mesh screen.*

all seed sold is grown by major contract growers in large fields in California or in foreign lands. The mature seed is shipped to packers, who then retail it for the next growing season—some sell from racks in garden centers and some by mail. However, mail-order seed is generally available before garden centers have begun to display seed packets. Also, catalogs on the whole offer a greater variety of seed than can be displayed on racks; it is simply a matter of space.

Before ordering from a catalog, take time to read descriptions. These helpful guides are designed to give all sorts of details to aid you in selecting the best seed and plant varieties for a successful garden. Here are some things to note when ordering vegetables.

Days to maturity. How long does it take the plant to develop ripe fruit? (The figure after the variety name in a catalog is the number of days to maturity. Days are counted from the date seeds are sown in the garden or, if started indoors in flats, from the date the seedlings are planted outdoors.)

Resistance. What diseases or pests can the plant resist or tolerate by itself? In many catalogs, abbreviations after the variety name indicate resistance; these are usually spelled out in the general information. (For example, *V* indicates the plant has resistance to verticillium wilt and *F* means to fusarium wilt; *N* refers to nematodes; *HWT* means it has been hot-water treated to kill fungus.)

Size and yield. How much room does the plant need to grow for maximum production, and does it produce all at once or in staggered amounts over a period of time?

Flavor. What is the fruit's taste; is it suitable for canning or freezing?

Acceptability. Will the plant perform well in most parts of the country or does it grow only in specific areas?

Seeds or plants. Some vegetables, such as peppers or tomatoes, need a long growing season, and in short-season northern climates, these are best started indoors before the last frost date. Others, such as lettuce, radishes, and beans, requiring fewer days to maturity, are sown directly into the garden.

STARTING SEEDS

Once my seed orders arrive in February or March, I begin to sow flower and vegetable seeds in the growing house of my large greenhouse. This is a time-consuming process; seedlings will not be ready for transplanting into the garden for two to three months. Starting seeds indoors is the best method for expensive seeds and for seeds that take a long time to germinate and grow, including most perennials as well as annuals, vegetables, and herbs such as basil and parsley that you want to start while the ground outside is still too cold or wet.

If you don't have a greenhouse and you plan to use window light, you will need to supplement it to

give your vegetable and flower seedlings a good start indoors. In January or February, even my south windows give only about six to eight hours of natural light. It is necessary to supplement this with ten to twelve more hours under fluorescent-light tubes; seedlings require about eighteen hours of light for proper growth—even more than mature plants. Keep the light tubes as close as possible to the leaves, but never touching them. Young seedlings will stretch toward the light source and must be turned daily to prevent them from becoming leggy. Replace your tubes when they reach 70 percent of their stated life service or, in any event, when the ends start to darken; by that time, they'll give about 15 percent less light than when new.

I sow seeds in plastic or wood flats about four inches high; be sure there are holes in the bottom for drainage. (Discarded egg cartons are a cheap alternative to flats.) Fill them about three-quarters full with a mixture of one-half sterile potting soil and one-half perlite or vermiculite. Mark off rows about two inches apart in a straight line with a pencil, pushing into the soil about one-half inch deep. (Be sure to check instructions on individual seed packets for more precise instructions. Some kinds need light in order to sprout and must merely be pressed into the soil surface, not covered with medium.)

I suggest planting one kind of seed per row and using garden markers to label each row. Cover the seeds lightly with soil medium and gently dampen with a fine spray so as not to wash away the seeds. Cover the surface of the flat with a pane of glass or clear plastic to keep in moisture. Put the flats in a warm spot but not in direct sun. (Check the packet, as some seeds prefer cooler germinating conditions.)

Try to resist peeking for four or five days. In about a week, little seedlings should appear. When they've come up about half an inch, remove the covering and move them into filtered sunlight. At this time, they are still too tender to take full sun. In another eight to ten weeks, they will be ready to be transplanted to the garden.

In case you are not yet aware, many new, ingenious shortcuts exist to using flats for germinating seeds. You can buy seed starter kits made up of nutrient-filled containers with the seeds already planted. All you do is remove the lid of the container, and water.

I also use peat pots—molded from peat and wood fiber. Seedlings started in them can be planted, pot and all, in the ground at the proper planting time. The roots will grow right through the soillike pot walls. Even easier are pellets made of compressed peat enclosed in plastic netting; soaking in water expands these ready-to-seed containers. As with peat pots, the pellet-container is planted right in the ground. When using these pots or pellets, remember that the seedlings growing in them dry out more quickly than do seedlings in flats. *Water regularly.* While they are a bit more expensive, I really think these new methods are the best—they make starting seeds extremely easy, and I suggest you try them.

Try to use all the seeds you order within the year. It is best not to save leftover seed, as this almost always results in poor germination.

Follow planting instructions on packets carefully. Sowing seeds too deep can contribute to poor germi-

LEFT: *This flat of cabbage seedlings, grown in my greenhouse, will plant a sizable block of earth in the kitchen garden. In the background, pots of calla lilies coming into bloom will be placed on display in the house.*

ABOVE: *All kinds of flower and vegetable seeds can be started in a fluorescent-light garden, with the tubes placed six to twelve inches directly above the leaves. A fluorescent growing area can be set up in a spare room or the basement.*

nation; if you are unsure of the depth to sow seeds, simply cover them lightly with soil. And always remember the two most important factors for germination—proper moisture and temperature. Too much or too little of either can spell only disaster.

Greenhouse Gardening

If you don't already have a greenhouse, I strongly suggest investing in some type—this is the only way to have flowers and even vegetables during the winter months if you live up north. Your greenhouse can be, but doesn't have to be, a large, commercial-style one like I have. A number of things are possible to do, in various price ranges, to create the desired environment.

On the south side of your house, you can construct a small lean-to greenhouse that utilizes the heat from indoors. This is not expensive and works well for overwintering plants, forcing bulbs, and starting seeds. If you're on a really tight budget, convert the sunniest window on the south side of your home into a small window greenhouse. This arrangement can be very enjoyable, especially if you hang bird feeders right outside. You can sit inside in comfort and observe your plants with the birds feeding only a few feet

LEFT: *A group of hybrid geranium seedlings in peat pots.*

RIGHT: *Hybrid geraniums from seeds come into bloom in four or five months, are virus-free, and therefore are more vigorous than those grown from cuttings.*

LEFT: *With a greenhouse, you will be able to have bulbs such as these Dutch amaryllis that come into bloom a few weeks after potting and placing in a warm spot.*

RIGHT: *This watercress growing in the greenhouse needs constant moisture, so I leave the pot standing in a deep saucer of water.*

away. Do-it-yourself greenhouse packages can be ordered through your local garden center or nursery.

I feel so strongly about having a greenhouse because I like to have flowers in my house all year long, especially in winter, when it's so cold and dismal outside. With a greenhouse—no matter what size or kind—you will be able to grow amaryllis and precooled spring bulbs (such as tulips, narcissi, hyacinths, and crocuses) during the dreary months. And, I love pre-cooled bulbs because they are easy to grow and their fragrance can be intoxicating, especially on a cold, sunny morning as you step into the greenhouse or room where they are blooming.

In the beginning of winter, your greenhouse becomes the center of gardening activity. The easiest vegetables to grow in a greenhouse in winter are watercress for salad and miniature vegetables in pots, such as tomatoes and cucumbers. We always start several pots of parsley in late summer, and it is ready for picking from Thanksgiving on. (If you dig and pot parsley that has been growing in your garden all sum-mer, be sure to bring it inside before frost, otherwise the plants will be misled into "thinking" it is their second season, which is when parsley, a biennial, concentrates all its energy in sending up tall flowering stalks.) A sunny, warm place in the greenhouse, or in a window garden, will also accommodate pots of rosemary, sage, thyme, and cilantro, or Chinese parsley (the last started

from coriander seeds planted in pots in late summer).

By January, everything in the greenhouse is more or less resting. Your main concern is to keep plants watered, clean, and insect-free. All yellow leaves should be picked off and discarded; clean, sweep, and rake your greenhouse to make sure fallen leaves don't create a hiding place for unwanted insects. Keep your eyes wide open for slugs and eliminate them as quickly and thoroughly as possible. I don't believe in using chemicals, but I am continually on the lookout for mealybugs, whiteflies, and aphids, and I spray with an organic insecticidal soap, when needed; organic controls are available at nurseries and garden centers throughout the United States.

Spring in Winter

In February, I like to get the feeling of springtime in the house by cutting forsythia branches for forcing. I choose branches with many flower buds—rounder and fuller than leaf buds. It's best to do this after a winter warm spell of a few days, not when the branches are frozen solid. I force the buds into bloom by placing the branches in a vase of warm water. It's fun to watch the flowers open slowly over a period of a couple of weeks in the warmth of the house. Besides forsythia, I also enjoy cutting and forcing branches cut from flowering crab apple, flowering cherry, and quince.

Houseplants

You can always find a plant to thrive in whatever indoor gardening space you have. The right plant in the proper place can change a room and alter the mood of the people in that room. Most indoor environments, however, are not specifically designed for plants, so it's up to you to choose plants that can best adapt to your indoor surroundings.

If you have rooms with lots of sunlight, your job is a cinch. The challenge is to find plants that will complement and highlight dreary, dark areas. Four important factors to consider when deciding which plants go where are light, temperature, water, and humidity.

Light. Most plants need some sunlight to produce flowers. The low-light ones, such as snake plant *(Sansevieria)* and pothos, or devil's ivy *(Epipremnum)*, rarely produce flowers but are treasured as beautiful foliage plants the same as Chinese evergeen *(Aglaonema)*, spider plant *(Chlorophytum)*, cast-iron plant *(Aspidistra)*, grape ivy *(Cissus rhombifolia)*, dumbcane *(Dieffenbachia)*, dracaena, mosaic plant *(Fittonia)*, and resurrection plant, or creeping moss *(Selaginella)*. When I want flowers in a low-light area, I rotate plants every two weeks, bringing them into the space already in bloom. Sometimes I use vases with cut flowers,

LEFT: *My favorite branches for forcing are forsythia. Here, they've burst into quite a celebration in the bay window of my dining room.*

ABOVE: *Cut branches of flowering quince in my entry hall. Each day, the buds swell until they push aside their brown jackets and turn into a preview of spring.*

RIGHT: *Flowering quince comes in both vivid and paler colors and looks especially beautiful against a gray winter sky. The branches themselves have a distinctive shape and line suggestive of Japanese floral decorations.*

replacing them once a week and changing the water every other day.

In a room with indirect light, such as filtered western, eastern, or northern exposures, the plants that do best are philodendrons, ferns, palms, ficus, German ivy *(Senecio),* ponytail plant *(Beaucarnea recurvata),* arrowhead *(Syngonium),* Norfolk Island pine *(Araucaria),* seasonal-flowering primrose *(Primula),* and forced bulbs, such as narcissus. For office environments with bright fluorescent light but no direct sunlight, try wax-leaf begonia *(Begonia semperfloreus)* or the lucky clover plant *(Oxalis regnellii).*

Southern exposures where light is filtered through curtains, blinds, or trees are ideal for flowering plants such as orchids (my favorites), azaleas, clivias, camellias, cinerarias, lipstick vine *(Aeschynanthus),* and some cacti. If your preference for these areas is not flowers, try devil's ivy, jade plant *(Crassula argentea),* wandering Jew *(Tradescantia),* Chinese fan palm *(Livistona),* coleus, or ferns.

If the room you're decorating has full sunlight, then you can grow almost anything. Some striking flowers to pep up a room are bird-of-paradise *(Strelitzia),* passionflower *(Passiflora),* lantana, large hybrid gloxinia *(Sinningia),* bougainvillea, chrysanthemum, jasmine, and for fabulous fragrance, gardenia. For simple elegant color, I like hibiscus, geranium *(Pelargonium),* and kalanchoe.

Temperature. Most plants prefer a cooler environment than what humans like. Generally speaking, plants flourish within a temperature range of 60 to 65 degrees F (15 to 18 degrees C). Geraniums, citrus trees, and ivy especially like cooler temperatures. More moderate temperature lovers, from 65 to 70 degrees (18 to 21 degrees C), are wax-leaf begonias, podocarpus, azaleas, strawberry-geraniums *(Saxifraga stolonifera),* piggyback plants *(Tolmiea),* pothos, waxplants *(Hoya),* and Norfolk Island pines. Some plants even do well in warm rooms of 70 degrees (21 degrees C) or more;

these include gloxinia, spathiphyllum, anthurium, cactus, dracaena, croton *(Codiaeum),* schefflera, dieffenbachia, and philodendron. If you must keep a room warm during the day, at least turn down the heat at night to benefit your plants.

Water. Watering is an age-old problem—the worry of many a gardener. There is no one rule for watering all plants, but here is a basic guideline: water to saturate the plant's roots when the soil surface feels dry. Use enough water so that it runs through the soil into the saucer under the pot, but never allow the roots to stand in water, as they will rot. Be sure you have the right equipment—a long-necked watering can is ideal—to make watering easy for you. I have several watering cans and especially like the newer, lightweight, plastic ones that come in attractive colors and will never spring a leak, at least not from rusting out.

Humidity. This is the most difficult to assess, as it is invisible; but, lack of humidity can result in parched, damaged foliage. If your house or office is dry, you can always add a humidifier to the room, or do as I do and use an atomizer spray of water once a week to moisten and revitalize my plants while at the same time cleaning the leaves. This is ideal for glossy-leaved plants; however, for my fuzzy-leaved plants, such as gloxinias, African violets *(Saintpaulia),* and Cape primrose *(Streptocarpus),* which are prone to getting water marks on the leaves, I use lukewarm water and always avoid splashing the leaves with water cooler than room temperature; the leaves may be dusted with a small, soft paintbrush. However, the humidity for these plants can be raised by resting them on a layer of wet gravel or sand in a tray.

How to begin. If you're a novice with houseplants, keep this list of easily cared for houseplants on hand when making choices: spider plant, grape ivy, cast-iron plant, dracaena, philodendron, piggyback plant, fern, ponytail plant, snake plant, jade plant, lipstick vine, wandering Jew, and waxplant.

In a room with full sunlight, you can
grow several different and sweet-smelling
jasmines such as this one, Jasminum
nitidum, *which blooms off and on all
year long.*

Orchids such as this vanda flourish in
southern-exposed rooms with filtered
sunlight.

Aloe is a plant that I believe ought to be cultivated in every household, since it's extremely easy to grow under ordinary house conditions and, furthermore, is useful! When a leaf is broken off, the gelatinous pulp that "oozes" from it is the perfect treatment for skin burns. This succulent will thrive in a sunny east, south, or west window and will survive in north light. Just be sure you use a soil mix suitable for cactus. Water when soil surface feels dry and pour off any excess water that drains into the saucer an hour after watering.

To start new plants, take cuttings from your favorites, or from ones that have become spindly and are ready to be cut back. Plants that grow upright with long stems, such as geraniums and begonias, can be propagated by stem cuttings. With a sharp knife, snip off healthy, upright-growing shoots several inches long

LEFT: *No household is complete without an aloe plant.*

ABOVE: *A purple florist gloxinia sprouts from the back of a ceramic rabbit.*

RIGHT: *I never seem to have enough geraniums, which is what you see me checking over here in a sunny bench of my growing house.*

with a few leaves. Root them in clean, sharp sand, perlite or vermiculite, available from any garden center. Sterile conditions, warmth, and humidity are essential for successful propagation.

Try raising houseplants from seed. This rewarding hobby demands little expense and only a small amount of time. You can have all sorts of delightful varieties of plants in every size, shape, color, and fragrance. African violets, aloes, cacti, cinerarias, fuchsias, geraniums *(Pelargonium),* gloxinias, impatiens, kalanchoes, primroses, and wax-leaf begonias, can all be started from seed. Follow procedures for germinating precious and small—some dust-size—seeds and be sure to use plant markers to keep the names straight.

When your seedlings grow to a few inches high, pot them up. A good potting mixture that I use for houseplants consists of:

    one part sterile potting soil
    one part coarse vermiculite or perlite
    one-half part coarse builder's sand
    with a little dehydrated cow or sheep manure.

Mix and add the following for each six-inch pot you use:

    one tablespoon dolomite or ground limestone
    one tablespoon time-release fertilizer, such as
        Osmocote
    one tablespoon bonemeal.

Another choice is a commercial sterile potting soil, such as Pro-Mix, available at nurseries and garden centers. It's premixed, so all you do is premoisten it well with warm water, then pot up your tiny treasures.

TOP: *Orchids are remarkably free of insect pests, but even they can fall prey to the likes of scale, mealybugs, and those dreadful slugs! Here you see scale insects imbedded in the surface of a cattleya orchid leaf.*

MIDDLE: *Sponging houseplants with lukewarm, soapy water (or a solution of water and insecticidal soap) at monthly intervals keeps deadly pests in check. But remember, you must be thorough* and *consistent!*

BOTTOM: *If not checked, the cottony mealybug will devastate the host plant. When the infestation is advanced, use a cotton swab dipped in rubbing alcohol to remove as many of the insects as possible. Then, spray with insecticidal soap. Mealybugs and other scale insects move around from plant to plant, even though we may not see them in action. They also have a survival tactic of proliferating on plants at the back of the bench where you may not see them. Be vigilant!*

Repotting. As your plants grow and thrive, they will require repotting into larger containers. When your plant needs a new home, select a new pot about two inches wider and deeper than the old one. Water plants the night before repotting to loosen up fine root hairs along the pot sides. Have all materials, including the potting mix and new container, ready. Most gardeners prefer clay pots, but plastic and glazed crockery are just fine as long as they have drainage holes.

To free the plant from a clay container, tap the pot against a solid surface to loosen the root ball. Plastic pots may be squeezed gently to dislodge the plant. Hold smaller pots upside down over a sink or receptacle with the fingers of one hand on either side of the plant and strike the bottom with the flat of your other hand, allowing the plant and root ball to slide out gently into your hand. With large, heavy plants, spread newspaper on the floor and ease the root ball out on its side. Never yank a plant out of its old pot by the stem. Be gentle with all plants; they'll appreciate it.

Be sure to add a layer of crocks (clay pot shards) or gravel at the bottom of the pot to improve drainage even with a good potting mix and in a container with drainage holes. Support the root ball with your hands and lower the plant into its new pot on top of a layer of fresh soil mix; make certain the plant sits at the same level relative to the top of the new pot as it did in the old one.

Fill in with soil mix, firming with your fingers. Water well. Keep the newly repotted plant out of direct sunlight for several days until it settles into its new dwelling.

Care. Pick off all dead flowers and leaves, as these are great hiding places for insect pests. Make it a habit to inspect all houseplants weekly and sponge them with lukewarm, soapy water at monthly intervals to check for such deadly pests as red spider, mealybugs, and scale. Infested plants must be segregated until bug-free! Any that simply cannot be saved must be thrown out promptly.

Avoid intolerable conditions that stress plants. Hot, dry rooms will kill anything, and hot or cold drafts will make plants lose their leaves and buds. Most houseplants, especially foliage ones, come from tropical climates, where they're accustomed to a *humid,* warm environment. Our apartments or houses, particularly during winter months, are often too dry, too dim, or too cool.

The number one problem gardeners have in taking care of houseplants is overwatering, which often results in "root rot." Yellowing leaves, stunted growth, brown leaf tips or margins, leaf loss, or the wilting of the entire plant may indicate overwatering. Waterlogged roots die simply because they can't breathe and do not get sufficient oxygen! Pots without drainage holes or with heavy, sticky soils are prone to this problem. Too much water will change roots from vigorous, healthy, white-tipped fibers to slimy, brown threads with blackened tips.

When roots become waterlogged and are dying, it is often best to accept the loss of your plant. However, if your favorite plant suffers from this complaint, try taking a cutting from the healthiest part and start a healthy new one.

Brown leaf tips can mean more than root rot. Paradoxically, they can also result from underwatering. Or, when furnaces fire up in winter and the humidity in your house or apartment drops, the margins of tender-leaved plants, including ferns, may turn brown. If you keep the plants away from vents, heat ducts, and radiators and stand the pots on wet gravel or sand in trays, they should revive. Better still, move stressed plants into the kitchen or bathrooms, where the air tends to be more humid. Leaf-tip browning can also be caused by a shortage of potassium. Although less fertilizer is required in winter than during the growing season, one or two feedings are a must to keep your houseplants flourishing.

Yellowing and dropping of leaves can mean many things. Pale, yellow, small leaves and slow growth can signal too little sun. But remember, every plant has its own best light level, and too much light can be as bad as too little. Often, leaves turn yellow and drop because your plant has outgrown its pot and the roots have become pot-bound. And, just like you and I, your plant can become stressed, and its leaves turn yellow and fall off, after a move from one environment to another. Just pamper it a bit by being sure the soil is nicely moist, neither wet nor dry; sit tight, and you'll both pull through.

Leaf spots can be caused by environmental stress or by fungus. Most fungal leaf spots have sharp outlines and are often covered with tiny black dots (fungal fruiting bodies). When you see these, immediately isolate the diseased plant from your healthy ones. Remove and destroy infected leaves. Never mist diseased plants and avoid splashing water on leaves. Most fungi travel through water, seeking openings for infection.

Poor air circulation and humid conditions, combined with hot daytime and cool nighttime temperatures, can cause powdery mildew—white patches on the leaves and flowers of your houseplants. Remove mildew-covered leaves and improve air circulation around the plant. If this fails, and you are very attached to your plant, you can try dusting with horticultural sulfur—a so-called environmentally safe fungicide—but read the directions carefully.

A word of caution. Most people do not know which portions of some common houseplants or which entire plants as well as outdoor ornamental shrubs are extremely toxic and, therefore, dangerous! Tiny children often put plant parts into their mouths, while toddlers will eat and drink whatever is available to them to satisfy their "taste buds." Please take the following special precautions if you have small children in your home.

Keep plants out of toddlers' reach.

Record the botanical and common names of each plant right on the pot or container for quick identification.

Know the number of the nearest "Poison Center" (look it up in your local telephone directory) and post it next to your telephone so you can call immediately if you have a problem.

Remember that small children are curious. Touching, smelling, and tasting are a natural part of learning. Children are more likely to reach out for plants or household products that have: a bright color; a strong, pleasing fragrance; an appealing taste, especially sweet; or an attractive label. Eighty percent of all poisonings involve children under the age of five.

Brightening Winter with Flowering Houseplants

When you're ready for spring, but winter is still dragging on, some indoor flowering plants can do wonders until you are able to get back to your outdoor annuals.

The flowering period for many beautiful plants—such as cyclamen, hydrangea, azalea, cineraria, and pocketbook plant *(Calceolaria)*—can be extended by turning the light up and the heat down. Bright window locations and cool temperatures are the key. These plants enjoy daytime temperatures of 60 to 65 degrees F (15 to 18 degrees C) and cooler nights, from 50 to 60 degrees F (10 to 15 degrees C); try moving them to a cool porch or basement at night.

Cyclamen can bloom for up to four months under these ideal conditions. Beautiful butterfly-like white, pink, lavender, or red blossoms last two to three weeks each. Bright, diffused light encourages bud development. Water plants thoroughly when the surface soil is dry to the touch; frequent watering is important, since wilting may damage buds. Take care never to let water stand in the crown of your plants, as this encourages rotting.

Hydrangeas will seem to last almost indefinitely if they are kept cool in bright, filtered light. Always protect flowering plants from direct rays of hot sun, from all drafts of air, hot or cold, and keep hydrangea supplied with lots of water—it's especially thirsty while in bloom.

Exotic chrysanthemums such as this orange spider need bright sun for buds to open; then, they can tolerate less light. Temperatures on the cool side help them last longer as houseplants. After bloom, varieties such as this are cut back and rested under a bench in the greenhouse until early spring, at which time they are watered, fertilized, and encouraged to grow new shoots for cuttings.

Chrysanthemums will bloom indoors in more moderate temperatures, up to 75 degrees F (24 degrees C) during the day and 70 degrees F (21 degrees C) at night. Cooler nights, down to 60 degrees F (15 degrees C) or less, will extend the three-week flowering period. Blossoms can be white, gold, yellow, pink, lavender, bronze, or red. The most common flower shape is classified as "decorative," with double blooms of long, curving, straplike petals. This is only one of many shapes; others include single, daisylike flowers; small, globular pompoms; those with spoon-shaped petals; and spider mums, with tubular petals. Bright light is essential for buds to open, but once in full bloom, mums can tolerate less light.

African violets can be coaxed into bloom in winter. As days grow shorter, the same windowsill where your violets flowered all summer may not provide enough light to keep them going. To flower, violets need bright, reflected light all day or full morning sun two to five hours daily—too much can cause "sunburn," unsightly yellow and brown splotches. If your window is no longer bright enough in winter, add artificial light. A combination of one generic "cool white" and one generic "warm white" fluorescent tube in the reflector fixture is the most economical and works well, so long as the tubes are no further than eighteen inches from the plant. Special plant-growing fluorescent lamps and a variety of decorative incandescent spotlights can also supplement natural daylight to boost your bashful violets back into bloom. Remember to use only luke-warm water; as with all fuzzy-leaved plants, splashed cold water will cause unsightly spots on the leaves.

Kalanchoes are the perfect choice for forgetful waterers, as these colorful succulents like to be kept on the dry side. Red, pink, salmon, white, orange, or yellow flowers blossom for six weeks and more all through the fall and winter months above thick, decorative leaves—attractive in their own right. A sunny location will keep colors bright; pale and bi-colored flowers indicate too little light.

Persian violet *(Exacum)* can bridge the gap between late winter and spring. Sporting fragrant violet-like blossoms in blue, purple, or white over a bushy mound of shiny, oval leaves, this plant can flower up to a month indoors on a bright windowsill and then bloom on for several months when placed outdoors in a partly sunny location.

For something more unusual—try tree-form geraniums or lantanas. Keep in mind that many flowering plants rest during the winter months of December, January, and February. Wax-leaf begonias and shrimp plants, however, are two houseplants that can give continuous bloom indoors on a sunny windowsill; also African gardenia *(Mitriostigma)* and Sambac jasmine *(Jasminum)*.

Many lovely prepotted bulbs, available at garden centers, are especially cultivated to bloom at Christmas-time. You can also start your own bulbs, including paper-white narcissus, hyacinth, amaryllis, and crocus, to bloom whenever you wish. These can last several weeks and require only a little watering every day or two. Many are extremely fragrant. When starting your own, try to find precooled bulbs or ask your garden center how long a cool period is required before they can be potted for indoors.

Early Winter Gardening Calendar

If you're an avid gardener like I am, this may be the only time you have to rest. Once the vegetable garden has been cleaned of debris, the compost pile turned, and the strawberries mulched, there's little left to do. There's not much to do for the lawn either, other than keeping off of it when it's wet or frozen; and, if you haven't dug up the geraniums and brought in the houseplants by now, chances are they will never forgive you. It's also likely that the seed companies have found you—so there's probably no need to write for catalogs.

LEFT: *Beautiful red and white cyclamens brighten a long, gray winter.*

BELOW: *It appears that Diana, goddess of the chase, has a winter stole, so that she is warmed and protected even in the midst of a snowstorm.*

RIGHT: *When snow falls, particularly icy snows, carefully shake off heavy loads that could break branches. Here, my dog Tiger—with his full winter coat that makes him look like a wolf—and I are out inspecting the yew topiaries and hedges after an unusually heavy and wet snow.*

They will be in your mailbox before you know it. So, other than planning for next year's gardening season, the gardener who just must garden will have to look harder for something to do.

OUTDOORS

Some trees and shrubs, such as fruit trees and most rosebushes, can be pruned throughout the dormant season.

Once the ground has frozen, a two- to four-inch mulch of straw or evergreen prunings can be placed over perennial beds to keep the ground from thawing and refreezing, which can result in frost heave and harm your plants.

Wrap wide-spreading evergreen shrubs gently with twine to prevent damage from heavy snows. When snow falls, particularly icy snows, carefully shake off heavy loads.

On warm days, when the ground thaws, water
your evergreens liberally to prevent winter leaf damage.

Broadleaf evergreens, such as rhododendron,
holly, and mountain laurel, if growing in an exposed
site and consistently damaged in winter, may benefit
from an application of an antidesiccant. Shading them
with burlap or snow fencing also helps.

If you have a live Christmas tree, plant it outdoors
soon after the holidays in a predug hole.

Be kind to all your plantings, including your
lawn, and use sand or kitty litter as a substitute for
rock salt.

INDOORS

There are so many indoor gardening projects; these
may include the maintenance and propagation of
houseplants or the start of something new.

Set up a system of lights for all those projects
you've wanted to do, like starting long-season vegetable
and annual and perennial flower seedlings or growing
flowering houseplants that require more light than
you have naturally.

Start a kitchen herb garden in a window with a
southern exposure or with artificial lighting.

Try the art of bonsai.

Force paper-white narcissus (no cold treatment
needed) or other bulbs for indoor bloom during the
late winter months.

Cut branches from early-blooming trees and
shrubs for inside your house and force them into
bloom.

Of course, rest and rejuvenation are a plus for
the gardener in winter.

NEXT COMES SPRING!

If you've followed my suggestions and are feeling
really ready and well prepared for the next season,
then all you can do is wait until it's planting time in
your area.

Daffodils collected from around my property and arranged for photography on a bed of baby Bibb lettuce in my kitchen garden show the range of styles and colors found among what botanists know as Narcissus.

$\mathcal{Q}$ Spring

Spring, without a doubt, is the most exhilarating time of the year. The thrill of springtime exists for everyone. And, for a gardener, this is the busiest season. After a long winter, whether you're starting a new garden or continuing one that's already established, you're eager to get going. There's lots to be done, and you'll have to hurry to keep pace with nature.

Tools

Before you begin planting, it is important to prepare your garden bed properly. Good garden tools are a must. All should be lightweight, preferably steel in one-piece construction, and comfortable to handle. I suggest a rake, hoe, shovel, pitchfork, hand-held pruners or clippers, and hose. Keep metal blades clean and oiled with machine oil, and they'll last a long time.

Soil

If you're starting a new garden, it is essential to know whether the soil is acidic, neutral, or alkaline as well as the measure of certain important nutrients. Usually the office of your county agricultural agent can test the soil for you or instruct you where to get this done. There may be a nominal fee. Check in the phone book under county government; the office is part of the U.S. Department of Agriculture.

The three most important minerals in soil are nitrogen, phosphorus, and potassium. You will want to test for these nutrients in your soil and for the pH (the measure of acidity and alkalinity on a scale from 1 to 14; a reading of 7.0 is neutral). Most plants prefer a neutral to slightly acidic soil. Your soil test analysis will give you a pH reading and nutrient levels and information on how to correct any imbalance in your soil.

Preparing Beds

I start preparing my garden in the fall for the following spring by spreading two to three inches of fertilizer—usually cow or horse manure, maybe some well-rotted compost—and rototilling it into the soil. This is also a good time to mix in any additives recommended in your soil test analysis. I then cover the garden with a mixture of shredded oak leaves and pine needles and leave it for the winter.

In the spring, when the ground has thawed, rototill the soil again thoroughly. Be sure the frost is really out of the ground and test your soil for workability before you start. Here's the test—squeeze a handful of soil; if it is too wet, it will clump damply; if too dry, it will flake apart. If it is neither too wet nor too dry, it will form a loose ball and then crumble apart when you press it ever so lightly with your thumbnail.

Turning over the soil will unearth insects that have wintered in your garden and expose them to sun and air, which will kill many of them—presumably the kinds you don't want and not the ones that are beneficial. The process also uproots pesky weeds. Keep

in mind that weeds are easily controlled when they're young and don't have a strong foothold in your garden; but, once established, look out. Clean the soil of weeds, pebbles, twigs, roots, or any other debris. After you have rototilled and mixed compost or rotted manure into the soil, rake the surface into a smooth, fine bed. Moisten the garden bed to the depth of at least six inches, better yet to one foot, and let it dry slightly before you begin planting.

UNCOMMON FERTILIZERS

Beginning gardeners often ask me about the benefits of using alternative fertilizers and mulches, and I tell them, being the game person I am, that I have tried some pretty unusual ones myself, including so-called zoo-doo. Several years ago, when Ringling Bros. and Barnum & Bailey Circus was in my town, I grabbed my shovel and filled several sacks with the "doo," offered free to anyone willing to come get it. I must say, the

LEFT: *Here are some of the tools I use for planting and gardening in general, from left to right: dibble, perennial spade, foot-operated bulb planter, small spading fork, trowel, edger, and combination trowel-cultivator. They are stored hanging on the inside walls of the toolshed that stands at the back of the kitchen garden.*

RIGHT: *The sight of primroses always signals spring, the thrill of which exists for everyone. These are a new, small-plant, large-flower development of* Primula x polyantha, *which I was asked to test for a seed company.*

By tulip time, in my kitchen garden all of
the beds are cultivated and ready if not
already planted.

RIGHT: Glorious tulips signify the beginning
of spring.

results were fabulous. The following year, my garden was superb. Scientifically, I haven't analyzed the digestive juices of wild animals, but when you consider that elephants and giraffes eat almost the same grasses as horses or cows, you would figure that the manure would be similar. However, lions and tigers, being meat eaters, would be completely different. I once received a letter from an eighty-year-old gentleman who lived in upstate New York; he told me about a circus his father ran in Times Square when he was a boy. The circus elephant, Dolly, became famous in his town upstate for supplying the region's fertilizer. As the story goes, the vegetables fertilized by Dolly were the biggest and the best anyone had ever seen.

Another uncommon fertilizer and mulch, usually readily available only to coastal gardeners, is seaweed, which must, of course, be treated to remove salt before use. To do this, make piles of fresh seaweed about one foot tall by four feet wide on a surface such as a gravel driveway that will allow the water to drain properly but won't be affected by the salt. Rinse the piles thoroughly and turn them three or four times over a period of several days to wash out all excess salt. Of course, a good day's rain will also go a long way toward solving any salt problems. After rinsing, you can add the seaweed directly to your compost pile. Seaweed, high in

I use printed labels for my garden beds that are easy to read and last from year to year.

TOP RIGHT: *Bean seedling lifts earth! Sounds like an amazing if impossible feat, yet that is what we ask all seedlings to do for us. It pays to prepare the planting bed well, to not cover too deeply, and to make certain the soil never dries into a hard crust.*

CENTER: *An old-fashioned wood hole marker comes in handy at transplanting time. It's best to give seedlings air space and room to flex so they'll grow strong.*

BOTTOM: *Here, I have direct-sown a bed of Bibb lettuce, my all-time favorite for salads when it is picked very young, at the "baby" stage.*

potassium and many minerals and with little cellulose, decomposes faster than leaves or hay; thorough rinsing does not remove significant amounts of its nutrients. If you wish to mulch with seaweed, you must first spread it to dry for about two or three weeks, after which you can then apply a three- or four-inch layer, shredded if you wish.

Planning and Planting

By now, the seeds you ordered in January have long since arrived, and by referring to your catalogs and the notes you made in winter, you know when and how to plant each variety. Be sure to also read the planting instructions directly on the seed packages.

Again, I want to stress the importance of having a plan before spring planting time arrives. Of course, my garden and greenhouses have been established for years, and my plan includes having cut flowers and plants in my house for the spring. In the fall and winter of the year before, I plant bulbs of tulips, daffodils and other narcissi, hyacinths, crocuses, and snowdrops. These can begin blooming as early as March on Long Island and continue into May. I bring them indoors as cut flowers or dig up the bulbs with some soil and pot them just as they are about to bloom. My favorites are the marvelously colored tulips such as the subtle Apricot Beauty or the almost glow-in-the-dark orange and yellow Easter Surprise, which bring the feeling of springtime right into my house.

Read carefully the notes you made over the winter for starting your new garden. In these, you should have listed what you want to plant and when. Your next important step, as you begin planting, is to keep good records.

Label your garden beds so you know what you planted where. Make rows about twelve inches apart for both flowers and vegetables. Sow seeds evenly down the rows and give your young seedlings ample

room to grow into maturity without crowding. First waterings should be very gentle, or you will wash the seeds away. In fact, one of the biggest hazards of spring is too much rain. Proper drainage in your garden beds is crucial; tender, new growth will drown if left standing in a pool of water.

TRANSPLANTING TIPS

Before actually transplanting your young seedlings into the garden, you will need to harden them off out-doors. Keep them moist and out of the sun for two days and then in filtered sun or a half day of sun for two more days.

Choose a cloudy day, if possible, for the actual transplanting. Seedlings may wilt or droop right after transplanting, especially if some roots were disturbed or broken in the process. First, take a group of seedlings (a small amount at a time) and place them on the soil surface, arranging them in a pleasing manner. Space them far enough apart so that each plant can grow to maturity without crowding its neighbor. Some require more space than others. Plants with the habit of branching from the base, such as lettuce, cabbage, pansy, petunia, the newer hybrids of zinnia and begonia, do not like their stems buried and should be planted so that the level of garden soil on the young seedlings is the same as it was in the pot. Other plants, such as tomatoes, peppers, marigolds, coleus, and impatiens, do not mind if the lower parts of their stems are below the soil surface; the buried portion of stem will send out roots.

An Annual Garden

Choose an area in your backyard that has good direct sunlight for an annual cutting garden. Some easy-to-grow flowers for beginning gardeners are zinnias, marigolds, Gloriosa daisies, cosmos, sunflowers, snap-dragons, larkspurs, and dianthuses—all of which are annuals easily grown from seed. To give your garden an extra touch, try strawberry plants—which have small leaves and flowers that resemble small, white, single roses—as a border. You can buy these at your local garden center, and you won't need many because the plants multiply. Eight plants would probably do, one at each corner and one in the middle of each row. Strawberry plants send out runners with new baby plants. In the fall, you can cut the runners and transplant the new strawberries next to their "parents." In a year, the perimeter of your cutting garden will be overflowing with strawberry plants, and you'll have the pleasure of fresh strawberries for summer meals.

LEFT: *Flowers of the future are part of my garden. Every season seed companies ask me to test new flowers for them. This frilly petunia is a fine example.*

An unexpected grouping of annuals glows in a basket.

Oriental poppies come in many colors, but my favorite is the clear orange Doubloon. After flowering in late spring, the coarse leaves turn yellow and die down, so it's best to plant them behind *some daylilies or another perennial that is leafy in summer. The oriental poppy roots can be transplanted in late summer or early fall.*

RIGHT: *Sweet William* (Dianthus barbatus) *is a true biennial: seeds started this year will bloom next season, and then the plants die. Despite the labor they require, I think their flowers are worth it for cutting.*

Growing Perennials

With all garden beds, soil testing and preparation is crucial, but particularly so with perennials, which will keep coming back year after year. When new gardeners ask my advice about establishing a perennial border that will require minimum care, I always suggest a combination of some of my favorite perennial flowers—primroses, peonies, oriental poppies, bearded irises, sweet Williams, daylilies, and chrysanthemums—to provide splashes of color from spring until fall. The primroses will flower first in early spring, followed by sweet Williams, peonies, irises, and poppies. With the right selection of daylilies, from which there are hundreds of colors and types to choose, flowers can last most of the summer and on into fall. The convenient thing about perennials is that when the flowers have finished blooming for the season and start to die back, you just cut the plants down to a few inches and forget about them until next spring, when they will sprout and bloom again.

A few other suggestions for spring color are forget-me-not, columbine, bleeding heart, and dwarf iris; for summer bloom, consider coralbells, hosta, phlox, lupine, and Shasta daisy; and for later summer on into fall, there are chrysanthemum, hardy aster, monkshood, Russian sage *(Perovskia atriplicifolia),* and black-eyed Susan *(Rudbeckia).*

Most perennials grow well in a sunny location, but there are some glorious ones for shadier spots. Many species of primrose, leadwort *(Pulmonaria),* bleeding heart, and columbine bloom in early spring in partial shade. *Epimedium* is another less well-known shade-tolerant perennial with spurred flowers; it also makes an excellent groundcover. Later in spring, peach-leaved bellflower *(Campanula persicifolia),* astilbe, and *Hosta* species (mainly grown for their attractive foliage) will thrive in shady conditions.

No matter what problem areas you have to deal with, there are perennials that will grow and bloom beautifully in them. Even damp areas with running streams can be ideal habitats for a wonderful range of perennial bog plants. Choose such plants carefully and be aware of just how big some can grow. Select plants for continual flowering and avoid color clashes, just as you would for a border. Some irises, including Siberian and Japanese varieties, will naturalize along the edges of streams and ponds. Others that will thrive in a moist environment are marsh marigolds *(Caltha);* some species of primrose; globeflower *(Trollius europaeus),* with rounded, golden yellow flowers; and that water-loving edible, watercress.

Although perennials—unlike annuals, which you must plant year after year—return each spring, most need to be divided every two to four years. How often you will have to do this depends on several factors, including the variety and soil and growing conditions.

Perennials should always be divided when dormant either before or after flowering. If a plant is lifted during its active growth period, it will likely wilt and die because of the extensive root disturbance. Generally speaking, perennials that bloom in spring or summer are best divided in late summer or early fall. At that time of year, it's most important that the plants have a couple of months to get established before winter sets in. If the perennials bloom late or if you have an early winter, separate them during their dormancy in spring. For more detailed information on dividing perennials, see "Fall," chapter 4.

Another method of propagation is by cutting. I often use this method with my hardy chrysanthemums. I take stem cuttings in late spring from plants that may be growing in pots in one of my greenhouses, or from those that live year round in the kitchen garden, and root them in sand. After two to four weeks, the cuttings should have roots and are ready to be transplanted into small pots filled with a commercial sterile potting soil. They can be set outdoors in spring in well-prepared beds when the frost is out of the ground. Set the new transplants no deeper than their original growing depth. Water well. Once the new plants have established themselves, in two to three weeks, give them a tiny pinch to encourage lateral shoots that will make the plant bushy. A last pinching can be done the middle of July—any later on Long Island, and the flower buds will not have time to set and bloom.

Some flowers grown as "perennials" are really not and need their own special care. Dahlias, although perennial in their native Mexico, are too tender to survive winters on Long Island. Their tuberous roots must be dug up each fall and overwintered away from freezing temperatures, where they will not dry out. The roots rot easily when injured or bruised. In March, I divide my dahlia roots with a sharp knife, selecting sections of tuberous root that have at least one eye or bud at the crown. If the "tubers" are still dormant and no eyes are visible, moisten the root clumps and place them in a warm spot for a few days until the small sprouts appear. Then cut and plant each root section horizontally, with the budded crown piece exposed in a flat of sterile potting mix or sand. Keep warm, moist, and in good light. When all danger of frost has passed, the well-sprouted roots can be planted directly in the garden or in pots for outdoors.

Not to brag, but my newest experiment with dahlias has been a big success—the tubers have been set in open spaces throughout the rose garden, wherever a bush might have died out. The soil, enriched by years of winter top-dressing with well-rotted horse manure from my stables, has supported strong growth and literally thousands of perfect flowers in many different colors and styles. They are staked my secret quick, easy, and effective way: a three-tier, circular wire tomato cage was inserted in the ground over each dahlia tuber after it was planted. All the growth shoots have just naturally entered their own little world inside the wire cage. They have required almost no individual staking and remarkably little breakage has occurred from windy, stormy rains.

Hollyhocks, another so-called perennial, are really biennial, which means they live for two seasons and usually bloom only in the second. Because hollyhocks self-sow liberally, they often create colonies in a garden that are perennial in effect. These lovely, tall, sun-loving flowers are a cinch to grow from seed. I sow them in a seed frame (which is simply a raised planting bed "hemmed" by four boards) in mid spring or right in the garden soil in late July or early August, and they are ready to bloom the following season. Some of the newer dwarf varieties will bloom the first year, so they

Large-flowered dahlias, such as this lavender, in the formal, decorative style often approach their fullest beauty at about the time of an early frost. I cover the plants the same as tomatoes so that their season can be extended through Indian summer. The individual cut flowers look beautiful in green bottles that once held wine; here, I have them on a table in my pool room with a sketch of me by Sir Cecil Beaton.

RIGHT: Cuttings may be rooted and seedlings may be started in any small pot, clay or plastic. I like to keep empty pots clean and stacked by size and kind so that they are ready when the moment arrives for transplanting.

Here I am in my mulched peony garden.
Winter mulch such as pine needles needs
to be raked off the peonies as the new
season's shoots appear in spring.

RIGHT: Here I am disbudding a peony
stalk of its smaller secondary bud.

FAR RIGHT: The "tree" peony called Age
of Gold blooms at an early age, with
large, double blossoms that are extremely
fragrant.

aren't true biennials and aren't likely, therefore, to return a second season.

Peonies are my absolute favorites among perennials. I love them so much I wish I could grow them at my winter retreat in Palm Beach, Florida, but unfortunately they require below-freezing temperatures and a period of dormancy not available in that climate. In more northern climates, gardeners use them beautifully in mixed perennial borders—they will even tolerate some shade.

One important thing to know about peonies is how to plant them. The crown from which the buds arise must be only one to two inches below the soil level—any lower and the plants will produce foliage but no flowers. I plant in early spring or fall—September and October are ideal, leaving ample opportunity for the peonies to become partially established before the first frost on Long Island. After a planting is well established, usually the second or third flowering season, as much as two-thirds of an individual stem can be cut for a bouquet; before that time, it is best when cutting the flowers to leave as much of the stem and foliage intact as possible, to support the plant itself.

If you want your peonies to produce larger blossoms, disbud the smaller secondary buds on each flower stalk; you will have only one flower per stalk, but it will be huge. Snip faded blooms to prevent seed formation.

I have a collection of Rothschild hybrid azaleas, a deciduous type having large flowers in flame colors, in front of my house.

RIGHT: Dr. Ruppel is a large-flowered hybrid clematis that originated in Poland. It blooms in late spring–early summer and requires little pruning. I train my clematis vines on tepees made from 4 six-foot wood tomato stakes (from the garden center) set at the corners of an eighteen-inch square and wired together at the top, then painted dark green.

FLOWERING SHRUBS AND VINES

"Tree" peonies, really shrublike in appearance, are one of my favorites in spring. These graceful beauties, native to Japan and China, are grafted today on herbaceous peony rootstock; but, unlike herbaceous peonies, the tree varieties have woody stems that do not die back with frost. Tree peonies are coming into favor with increasing numbers of gardeners, and more and more varieties are being offered in nursery catalogs. Plant them in fall, and be sure you set the union, where the tree peony is grafted to its herbaceous rootstock, about four inches below the soil surface.

Colorful masses of azaleas speak spring to many people. I always water well during drought conditions and mulch with oak leaves, pine needles, and peat moss to protect the shallow roots and maintain acidity. Azaleas are acid-lovers and thrive in soil with a pH around 5.5. The shrubs are shallow-rooted and require well-drained soil, but the plant roots should never be allowed to dry out. Early summer is the time to shape your azaleas if they need it. Because these spring-flowering shrubs set their buds for the next year's blooms by mid-August on Long Island, the time I prune is after July Fourth but before the end of the month. I also must protect my tender varieties from freezing, desiccating winds with burlap screens.

Another favorite of mine is clematis. Starting new plants from a neighbor's or your own is really very easy. For hybrid clematis that will not grow true from seed, air-layering is the method most gardeners find easiest. In spring, cut a two-inch slit at an angle between two nodes, but no more than halfway through the young shoot. First, wrap damp, long-strand sphagnum moss around the cut and then put clear plastic on top, securing the ends of the plastic to the stem with adhesive tape or twist ties. To prevent a heat buildup, which could kill or injure new growth, it's best to wrap burlap over the plastic. Roots will start to grow in about three to six weeks; then, sever the rooted section and transplant. This climbing vine will need a trellis to support its growth, and it does best with its roots in the shade and tops in the sun.

Species clematis, not hybridized varieties, can be grown from ripe seed collected in summer or fall. Store the seed in a plastic bag in the refrigerator crisper (not the freezing section) until spring or, if you prefer, sow the seed immediately in a flat indoors or in a prepared nursery bed outdoors. Water regularly until germination occurs, in two weeks to two months, depending on the species.

Clematis stems are highly vulnerable to breakage. One way to protect a young plant and also give its roots the cool shade it needs is to train all emerging shoots up through an overturned clay pot that has been mostly submerged in the soil. Notice that the original drain hole has been enlarged to accommodate the clematis.

RIGHT: *Large-flowered hybrid clematis such as Nelly Moser blooms profusely in late spring–early summer, then again in early fall.*

The formal rose garden enclosed by a brick wall just off the terrace has a statue of Diana, goddess of the chase, watching over.

The Templeton Garden

At Templeton, my main house on Long Island, I have two formal rose gardens and a large kitchen garden. Starting in early spring, I follow a very simple system each year. First, the roses are inspected, and all dead canes are pruned. If overwintering scales or other insects are found, on a windless day they are sprayed with a dormant oil (also called horticultural oil). All the climbing vines are staked, and any winterkill is removed. Next, the winter protective mulch is cleaned from the perennials, and the soil in the kitchen garden is tidied and prepared for spring planting by rototilling and raking. Most of this work is done in late March and early April in my area (Zone 7), but you must garden for the climate in which you live.

First, we plant the hardy and cool-season vegetables, such as lettuce and other salad greens, radishes, peas, onions, spinach, potatoes, Swiss chard, and cauliflower. Lettuce will bolt or set seed when subjected to warm temperatures and is, therefore, grown in spring and again in fall, during cooler weather. I generally sow seeds directly into the garden as early as mid-March. Any transplants are set out in my garden from mid-April to early May. Staggered sowings of lettuce seed, every ten days or so, will extend the harvest period.

A few weeks later in my area, the warm-season vegetables and annual flowers, which will come up blooming and ready for harvest by the end of July or beginning of August, go in. These include tomatoes, peppers, marigolds, zinnias, beans, pumpkins, watermelons, and eggplants.

I treat my perennial vegetables and herbs, such as asparagus, horseradish, rhubarb, chives, mint, sage, thyme, and tarragon, as I do perennial flowers; they have a permanent spot in my garden. I plant lettuce, string beans, peas, corn, carrots, basil, parsley, dill, and other annual vegetables and herbs yearly and rotate the beds every two to three years.

Perennials are the mainstay of my garden. They are there every spring, poking their little heads up toward the sun. In early spring, the tulips, narcissi, hyacinths, and other bulbs appear first. In late spring and early summer, the flowers of peonies, lilies, poppies, lupines, and delphiniums fill my garden with almost every color of the rainbow. Perennials fill vases in every room of the house throughout the spring season. When cutting flowers from tulips, narcissi, or other bulbs, cut the stem on a diagonal, halfway between the flower and the stem base. The remaining part of the stem and leaves is the food for next year's bulb growth. With herbaceous perennials, all you have

LEFT: *As it happens, my herb bed is sort of six-sided. Here, I have set out the beds for different herbs by using long bamboo canes; bark chips are in place to indicate the paths.*

RIGHT: *Glorious blue-purple delphiniums bloom in the late spring and early summer.*

Freesias perfume the air in a north window of my dining room.

My mother's kitchen garden provided every size, shape, and color of cut flowers that one could imagine, including bouquets of sweet peas that smelled heavenly to my childish nose.

to remember is that the more the flowers are picked or deadheaded (spent blossoms removed), the more they are stimulated to bloom.

Lilies (*Lilium* species and cultivars) are especially marvelous perennial bulbs, as varieties exist that bloom from May until the first frost in every possible shape, size, and color—and they are fabulous in cut-flower arrangements. Once cut, they can last for two or three weeks. It is best to cut your flowers in the morning or evening, not in the middle of the day, when they may be somewhat wilted. Always pick them when they are in bud or before they have fully opened— this preserves the life of cut flowers and their fragrance. I have found peonies, tuberoses, zinnias, marigolds, cosmos, Gloriosa daisies, and roses (cut while still in bud) last a long time in arrangements and are good for

Some of the tools needed for general tidying up and maintenance of the garden include, from left to right: a high-quality, nonkink hose; large and small metal (or bamboo) leaf rakes; garden rake; goatskin gloves; pruning shears; and a regular broom.

repeat cutting—which means when you put in fresh water, you also rinse the stems and recut them an inch or two shorter. I always pull off the lower leaves that will be below the water line and snip the ends of the stems at an angle so that the flowers can easily absorb water. Fresh-cut flowers require a lot of water, so it is important to keep a close check on the vase for the first day, adding more water if the level drops. Keep the water clean and fresh and place the arrangement in a cool place—never near a heat source, such as a radiator or vent. Some people use a commerical chemical additive or drop an aspirin in the water to prolong the life of the arrangement, but as far as I'm concerned, this isn't necessary.

My favorite flower arrangements are lovingly placed in a casual way that shows off the beauty of the individual blossoms—but without too much fixing. You may be shocked, but some of my most-used vases are empty and clean glass jars from instant coffee. I also appreciate bouquets with fragrance. I love to smell sweet scents in my house and garden. My favorites for indoor bouquets are daffodils, lilacs, peonies, roses, lilies, and freesias. Of course, the roses, lilacs, and all but the freesias grow outside in my Long Island garden. Freesias will grow in pots in the greenhouse and can be moved into the house. Some of my other most fragrant plants grow as houseplants or in the green-house: sweet olive *(Osmanthus fragrans)*; scented-leaved geraniums *(Pelargonium),* with odors including that of mint, rose, nutmeg, apple, lemon, and coconut; gardenia; jasmine; hoya; lavender *(Lavandula dentata*—a variety that does well indoors); lemon-verbena *(Aloysia triphylla);* and some cyclamen, including the new mini varieties. Another favorite of mine is hyacinth; the bulbs can be forced or brought indoors in pots from the garden when they are in bloom in early spring. The scent of narcissus, another easily forced bulb, is extremely heady.

I have no set design rules for arrangements. I love flowers separately or mixed together, and I find that most complement one another. Sometimes, I like to try daring combinations; for example, I'll mix different kinds of potted orchids with cut flowers to create wonderfully exotic arrangements.

By the first week in June, all my outdoor spring planting is finished, unless of course, it is a very unusual year. Starting in June, all the beds are cultivated once a week and the garden is kept raked and tidy.

Now is the time to implement a system to help you organize your time wisely so that you will be able to complete all the many, many tasks required to keep your garden healthy, attractive, and productive. I do this by designating each day of the week for a different, specific task in my garden.

Mondays at Templeton are for grass cutting and "the battle of the bugs." Of course, some weeks the grass grows faster than others, so I compensate and occasionally do an extra mowing or skip a week. I try to inspect and handle any insect problems on Mondays, but if I were to discover an infestation of slugs or white-flies on another day, I would handle it immediately.

Tuesdays are for weeding and mulching.

Wednesdays, Fridays, and Sundays, we water (depending on the amount of rainfall; sometimes we water less if we've had ample rain, and sometimes in August, I'll water every day—that is, if there are no drought restrictions).

Thursdays and Saturdays are for cutting, picking, and staking and for general tidying of the garden.

Develop your own system based on your own needs, but start in spring and continue until the garden is finished for the year. Once you set up a system and begin to implement it, you can always revise and modify to find what works best for you.

The important thing is to develop the system, and then stick with it!

Two different camellias cut from the greenhouse with a miniature cyclamen, in the window of the little dining room. The cyclamen has a light, lemony scent.

RIGHT: *The lady's slipper paphiopedilum and cattleya orchids shade a photo of the famous Templeton polo team of the late 1930s. From left to right: Michael G. Phipps, James Milles, Winston F. C. Guest, and Robert Strawbridge.*

Templeton House at the End of May

Decorating with flowers means more to me than just putting a pretty bouquet on a polished table. I give a lot of thought to the flowers I bring into each room—to make certain their color, fragrance, and shape enhance the decor of that space. I almost never purchase plants or flowers to bring into my home—they all come from my gardens and greenhouses. So, when I want to fix up the house, I begin by making a quick survey of what is ready to cut from the garden or to bring potted from the growing houses.

The small dining room. This small room, right off the pantry, has a fireplace that makes it a cozy space for private dining with family and close friends. Dark burgundy walls are covered with hunting prints and various game heads shot by my late husband, Winston. The dining chairs and banquette are covered in a salmon floral pattern designed especially for the Old Westbury Gardens. Here, I almost always have flowering plants on display in the windows—orchids, geraniums, streptocarpuses, calla lilies—and there may be large bouquets cut from spring-blooming trees and shrubs or big pots of my favorite large orchids, such as vandas and the imposing big hybrid laeliocattleya.

From outdoors, I cut delicate scarlet flowers with

yellow centers, white ones with yellow centers, and yellow ones with scarlet centers from my tree peonies. I arrange these using old Mateus wine bottles for vases. I combine pots of pink geraniums and pink hydrangeas from the greenhouse with pots of lovely feathery lavender astilbes. On the dining table itself, I like to have one or more bud vases, each holding one or more of the most exquisite blossoms that can be found—often one-of-a-kind treasures from the greenhouse.

The main dining room. Pale green walls are framed with baseboards and window trim that is marbleized a darker green. The walls are covered mostly with oil paintings of homebred thoroughbred race-

horses, and over the mantle is a big oil painting by Richard Stone Reeves of me and my children riding on our property.

I fill the windowsills with lovely burgundy and pale green paphiopedilum orchids. Pots of pale pink vanda orchids cover the console table in the bay window, and the sideboards are overflowing with yellow oncidium orchids.

The gallery, leading to the library and the front hall. The walls are the same colors and texture as the dining room, and on the floor is a leopard-pattern wool carpet.

Pots of white cattleya orchids decorate the win-

LEFT: *Pots of freesias and orchids are arranged in front of one of the oil paintings in the main dining room.*

RIGHT: *The spots on this rare Oncidium orchid are echoed on the leopard fabric in the library.*

BELOW: *Small-leaved English ivies train easily into five-inch wreaths I enjoy having on display close to where I sit in the library as well as in the windows of the gallery leading to the front hall. After a month or two, they go back to the growing greenhouse for R and R.*

dowsills. Sometimes I add miniature dwarf myrtle trees in four-inch metal copies of Versailles tubs painted dark green or five-inch wreaths of small-leaved English ivies in plain terra-cotta pots with matching saucers. There is one very large cachepot that sits on the floor along the wall opposite the door to the library where I may stand a shoulder-high vanda or a golden angel trumpet *(Brugmansia)* trained as a tree.

The library. The walls and banquettes in this room are covered in the same small-print green fabric with the same leopard-print carpeting as in the gallery. I love lavender orchids in this room, and I fill tall vases with red and white peony flowers. I spend a lot of

time in this room, and it is also where I am most likely to have a glass of wine at the end of the day with my closest friends, so the prettiest cut flowers and flowering potted plants are brought here, even when I may not have the time or inclination to fully decorate other rooms in the house.

The front hall. This is a wide and long space with the walls marbleized in my signature burnished orange, a color very akin to terra-cotta, which looks beautiful with all flowers and plants. I like big pots of flowers in this space—five-foot-tall staked orchid plants: scarlet renantheras, yellow dendrobium orchids, and peach-colored vandas. Also, I keep a pot of yellow-flowering

LEFT: *Tall, staked dendrobium orchids flank a large oil painting of my late husband's father, uncle, and aunt, who were painted, as children, in 1877; it hangs in the front hall.*

ABOVE: *I love to put lavender cattleyas or yellow and orange orchids in the library.*

White cattleya and pink dendrobium orchids embellish the pool room.

RIGHT: *At peony time, I can't resist filling the blue-and-white salon with big bouquets in all shades of pink.*

Carolina jasmine here on occasion, for its beautiful form trained as a pillar about twelve inches in diameter and five feet tall. I also have two very large sweet-olives that sometimes stand here flanking a rare species of camellia with white-edged, rose-red flowers that is nearly ten feet tall and about five feet in diameter.

The blue-and-white salon. The blue-and-white wool carpet sets the tone for this space, in which I use mostly white or blue flowers, with an occasional spot of pink. I find pots of white cattleya orchids add the right touch in spring, often with pots of blue and white African violets continuing from winter, as well as streptocarpus, which may be all white, all blue, or in stunning combinations of white and various blues.

The pool room. The pool table occupies almost one-half of this room. The rest is given to soft banquettes and easy footstools, all upholstered in off-white sailcloth. A couple of chairs are upholstered and a round table draped in a floral fabric created for the Old Westbury Gardens. The walls are painted terra-cotta, with white trellis panels that help make all flowers and plants placed here look as though they were in a glamourous winter garden. Orchids are my favorites here, too. I have a glorious mix of orchids in pots: dendrobium, cattleya, phalaenopsis, vanda, rhynchostylis, and schomburgkia. The wonderful yellow, scarlet, lavender, white, and orange tones breathe life into this room.

The large salon with the cathedral ceiling. The ecru walls are covered with large oil paintings of Phipps family members, including one of my late husband, Winston, painted by John Singer Sargent. At this time of year, my choices for this room are orchids and peonies. Yellow and brown oncidium orchids bloom in large pots, while beautiful white and pink peonies spill out of vases.

Now on to summer.

Cut hydrangeas stand up to their necks in cool water in a florist bucket set between Asiatic hybrid lilies for cutting that are grown in rows in the kitchen garden.

*Chinese trumpet lilies such as the Ana-
conda are prime candidates for staking,
as they can grow to five or six feet.*

3 Summer

By mid-June, you really start to see the fruits of your labor. Everything that you've planted is peeking through the soil, and your perennials are in full swing. Be sure to take the time to remove the faded blooms once they are spent; this process, called deadheading, prevents the plant's energy from going into seed production and will encourage new flower buds to form. All those tall, flowering beauties in your perennial border, such as hollyhocks, dahlias, delphiniums, lupines, and lilies, should be staked so they won't blow over or break in the wind.

At the beginning of summer, you've already been enjoying asparagus, lettuce, radishes, peas, and your other early-producing vegetables. In my garden on Long Island, the corn is ankle high at this time; it will need at least an inch of water a week to assure good production, which means watering during summer dry spells. Tomatoes, cucumbers, squash, melons, eggplants, and peppers are all still too small to snitch a bite, but it's hard to resist. Patience has never been one of my virtues.

Summer annuals begin to show promise; cosmoses, zinnias, marigolds, and China asters *(Callistephus chinensis)* will be ready for cutting in about a month. As the summer progresses, you'll get more and more enjoyment out of your garden, but don't think it's all fun—there's still a lot of work to be done. After the preparation and planting comes maintenance, and there are four essentials for maintaining your garden in excellent condition. You must be on the alert for insect pests and diseases and be vigilant in your watering and weeding.

The Battle of the Bugs

Plants are just like people. They have to be clean and healthy to feel good. Since your plants can't get up to take a bubble bath or visit the doctor for a shot of B12, it's your duty to be something of a nursemaid. Here are a few reminders for starting a healthy garden.

First, be sure your seeds, bulbs, and cuttings are clean and healthy when you buy them.

Second, when sowing seeds indoors, use a sterile medium. I like the seed-starting formula available from Burpee, but you can also pasteurize soil yourself in an oven. Bake it at 160 degrees F for thirty minutes to kill diseases, insects, and weed seeds; but I warn you, the odor created by baking soil is gamy, to say the least, so don't attempt this unless you have the best of ventilation systems.

Last, try to choose new varieties of vegetables, flowers, trees, and shrubs that have been bred to resist common diseases. That way, you won't have to worry about diseases causing your plants to suddenly wilt and keel over in the middle of summer. Check the latest seed and nursery catalogs for the most recent introductions.

If you follow these steps, your garden will be

Mid-June in my kitchen garden: Asiatic hybrid lilies and Goldenglow rudbeckias bloom in the foreground; white Hydrangea arborescens Annabelle grows in the background left, achillea Salmon Beauty at center—both plants I have been testing.

"One for the blackbird. Two for the crow. Three for the cutworm. Four to grow!" At the beginning of summer in my garden on Long Island, the corn is ankle high, and the first planting of green beans soon will be ready for picking.

Tall, large-flowered American marigolds, the Lady Hybrid series, for example, rank among the best annual flowers for cutting. The small-flowered and compact bushy Signet marigolds such as Lemon Gem make wonderful edgers and patio pot plants.

clean and healthy, helping to reduce the number of insect pests and diseases; but, of course, you can never totally eliminate them. As you begin the battle of the bugs, the first thing you can do is not to disturb nature's protective army. Birds, toads, lizards, and snakes are the good guys who feed on a wide variety of insect pests. I've always been lucky enough to have uninvited toads in my garden. As adults, these helpful creatures usually burrow into the ground during the day and feast at night on insects. During their breeding cycle, they require a lake or other water source in which to lay eggs and for the few weeks that they are tadpoles. If you have a lake nearby but no toads, you might try purchasing some in an aquarium shop or from a water garden specialist in spring or summer. Try encouraging your toad population to hang around; make an appealing haven by putting out small, flat aluminum pans of water and an overturned clay flowerpot in a cool, shady

FAR LEFT: *Follow my rule in the garden—no poisons—and the lizards will be your full-time workers, keeping plant-eating bugs at bay.*

BELOW: *A benevolent frog is on the lookout for dinner.*

LEFT: *Chipmunk caught in action! Unfortunately, it was only in the camera. These speedy and industrious creatures have decided my kitchen garden is The Place To Be in summer and that it is awfully nice of Mrs. Guest to provide warm greenhouses as their winter quarters. Getting cats is out of the question, owing to the sizable dog population at Templeton, so we've learned to ignore the chipmunks.*

Beyond the freshly turned soil in the foreground are rows of leeks; since they are members of the onion family, I will follow them with something like beans or lettuce, not onions or scallions.

place. I know many people are afraid of lizards and snakes, but believe me, there's no better bug terminator than a good green garden snake.

If your garden is not too big, I suggest daily inspection of each plant, and hand picking (with gloves on, of course) to remove all visible insect pests. A number of alternatives may be tried before spraying. For instance, if grasshoppers are a problem, you can try tilling the top three inches of your soil soon after the fall harvest to reduce the number of grasshopper eggs in the soil, or you might consider planting trap crops of coles such as cabbage and kale, which many grasshopper species find preferable to other vegetables, or use row covers on young seedlings. And, don't overlook nature's protective army; encourage birds—grasshoppers' natural predators—to stick around your garden with feeders, birdhouses, or a birdbath. Don't worry, even if these welcome guests start to make unwelcome advances on their own, such as nibbling small fruits or nipping the tips off just-sprouted beans, birds can easily be thwarted by draping garden netting over the temptations. They hate to have their feet entangled and will stay away from protected crops.

Sometimes, people write me asking how to rid their gardens of cats—birds' natural enemies. Keep in mind, though, that cats can be beneficial for controlling moles, mice, chipmunks, and rabbits in the garden. Cats, however, often have a nasty habit of using freshly dug beds as litter boxes. If mothballs or a dose of bloodmeal on the soil surface doesn't deter cats, then you could try a small dog, such as a terrier. A dog is also useful for scaring rabbits. Without one, you might disenchant rabbits from young shoots, flowers, and vegetables by dusting the tempting plants, when they are damp, with powdered lime, sprinkling them with red pepper, spraying with a solution of common brown laundry soap and water, or spraying with a solution of one-half cup of epsom salts in a gallon of water.

But, getting back to insects and their destruction of flowers and vegetables, I don't believe in the use of chemicals in the garden, although I sometimes use insecticidal soap sprays. The best spray in the vegetable and flower garden is organic, and if your stomach isn't too weak, you can blend your own daily concoction of bug juice cocktail! Collect about a cup of the insects that are attacking your crops and grind them in an old blender with two cups of water. Mix thoroughly, strain the mixture, and then spray it back on the crops. Bugs don't relish the idea of being sprayed with their "own kind." In fact, the spray will make all bugs almost as sick as it has made you.

Toxic chemical sprays not only pose risks to gardeners and harm helpful insects, they can also poison earthworms, sometimes called "nature's tireless little workers." Be happy when you come across earthworms; they aerate your soil by feeding on decaying organic matter, passing it through their intestinal tract and then back into the earth. To keep earthworms happy, healthy, and at work in your garden, make sure there is plenty of rich organic matter in the soil.

Diseases

Give your plants a good start in life. They need a spotless garden, as we have already discussed, good soil that is amply fertilized and drains well, mulching, and proper spacing. Under stress, plants are more prone to all kinds of diseases and insect pests.

Spacing provides ample sunlight and ventilation for all your plants. This helps to minimize unnecessary dampness, thereby discouraging fungal diseases, such as mildew, blight, and wilt. It also gives plant roots room to grow and flex their muscles a bit. Without good drainage, water can build up and become stagnant, causing root rot and weakening your plants.

To avoid the potential for a buildup of soil-borne

disease and even insect pests, rotate your vegetable crops every year or two, especially tomatoes and the coles or brassicas, crops such as broccoli, cabbage, and cauliflower. This rotation isn't important for flowers, but for vegetables, it is a must. It prevents the accumulation of insects and diseases that attack that particular crop. And don't forget about looking for those new disease-resistant varieties when you plant vegetables, flowers, and even trees and shrubs.

When disease is present, be very careful not to spread it through carelessness. Sterilize pruning tools used to remove diseased portions of plants. Wipe the blades with a solution of one part liquid bleach to nine parts water after each cut.

Take care, when you cultivate your plants, not to injure them. Some viruses enter plants through wounds made by careless handling, such as banging a lawn mower into a tree or whizzing into the trunk with a string-line trimmer. Remember, plants really are like people; they need to be handled with tender, loving care.

Watering

I have always felt that watering a garden correctly is a most difficult task for someone to learn. I don't know why, but new gardeners seem to be either dehydrating their plants or drowning them. In the hot summer months of June, July, and August, I follow a simple rule: keep the ground moist around the plants. You may have to water twice a day, morning and early afternoon, as well as use a heavy mulch to keep in dampness. But never water so much that your plants are standing in a pool of water; just keep the ground around your plants evenly moist.

The ABC's of watering are known to most of you, but here they are again.

—During the growing season, soak your plants for up to one hour every seven days or so—a good steady rain will accomplish this for you.

—Water in the morning, whenever possible, and never let your plants go to bed with water on their leaves, as this can cause fungal problems, such as mildew and blackspot in roses.

—If you are thirstier than usual, then maybe your garden needs a drink, too. Like you, your garden needs more to drink in hot months than in cooler weather.

In areas plagued by severe drought, it is essential to save water. The ideal method for watering during drought conditions or just to conserve water is to set up a drip irrigation system. The water goes directly into the ground with none of the evaporation and runoff (and the risk of spreading fungal diseases is drastically reduced) that takes place with overhead watering. A less complex way is to use a sprinkler soaker hose, with tiny holes on one side, and lay it so that the holes face the ground. The water will slowly trickle directly to the roots of your plants.

If a waterless summer is predicted, you can help your soil retain moisture better by adding extra organic matter, such as compost, leaf mold, or well-rotted manure, to it before you plant. Raise plants that can tolerate drought and heat best; some suggested varieties follow later in this chapter in "The Flower Garden" and "The Vegetable Garden" sections. When the plants begin to grow, surround them with a four- to six-inch mulch to further enhance moisture retention as well as to maintain a uniform soil temperature. Keep in mind, though, that a severe drought requires that even tolerant plants be watered, especially early in the season until roots can take hold. When leaves droop, the plant is wilting and needs water. Be sure to water soil, not plant leaves.

Trust me, one of the best things you can do is to acclimatize your plants; this is true at any time but especially during drought conditions and for young and tender plants raised indoors. This simple process involves gradually exposing the plants to full sun, drying winds, rain, and outdoor temperatures. Set your

The overhead sprinkling system in my kitchen garden working away and sparkling in the June light.

If at night your roses are sent to bed with water on their leaves, fungal problems such as blackspot can spread rapidly. If this happens, pick and destroy the most damaged leaves; then spray or dust with a rose fungicide.

Here is the kitchen garden in early July, with mature carrot "fern" in the foreground, perennials blooming at center, and thigh-high corn growing beyond.

RIGHT: *We use a variety of weeders and cultivators, including, from left to right: three- and single-tine cultivators, Cape Cod weeder, small hand-held rake, dandelion evictor, and Dutch hoe.*

tender plants in a protected semishaded location during a warm day and take them in at night. After several days, leave the plants outside day and night and begin the gradual process of exposing them to more and more sun and natural elements. When the plants have adapted to the outdoors, they are ready to plant. Water deeply after planting and continue regular watering until the plant is established, in about a week or ten days; then, water when necessary.

Weeding

A weed is an unloved, unwanted plant. Unfortunately, weeds are strong and aggressive and will take over a garden in no time if not kept under strict control. And, they can act as sanctuaries for many insect pests and diseases.

Rototill your soil deeply in spring to kill off as many weed seeds as possible before sowing your own flower and vegetable seeds. Then, as your garden grows, you must constantly weed, especially right after a rain. Pull out by hand any weeds that appear or remove them with a hoe just at the soil surface. Regular cultivation will inflict terminal damage on the shallow feeder roots of weeds, especially with plants that are growing vigorously, with extensive root systems. Once your crops are growing vigorously, mulch them with a layer of almost any organic mulch material that you may have on hand or can purchase. This will help keep the weeds down by blocking out the nourishing rays of the sun; it will also help retain moisture, insulate the roots of the plant from extreme temperatures, and when it breaks down, provide organic matter for the soil.

Some people use chemical weed control, but again I don't believe in this. Your garden will flourish if you tend it well, and a farmer will tell you that when healthy weeds can be grown on a patch of ground, that is a good sign that the soil there is worth working for crops. The weeds can be controlled by hand or with a simple garden hoe—all it takes is determination and perseverance! If you continue weeding all season, your reward will be bigger and better crops and fewer weeds in the next season.

The Flower Garden

As early summer progresses into late summer, the garden comes into its own. By August, annuals and summer-blooming perennials are in full bloom: lilies, hollyhocks, sunflowers, zinnias, marigolds, Gloriosa daisies, China asters, and cosmos.

For those of you who face severe heat or water restrictions, I have compiled a list of some drought-tolerant flowers.

First, the annuals: basil, catharanthus (also called annual vinca or periwinkle), celosia, cleome, cosmos, four-o'clock, gazania, globe amaranth, marigold, melampodium, morning glory, nicotiana, ornamental peppers, portulaca, sanvitalia, statice, strawflower, summer cypress *(Kochia)*, sunflower, and zinnia. All these heat- or drought-tolerant annuals can be started easily from seed.

Now the perennials: butterfly weed *(Ascelpias)*, coreopsis, gaillardia, lavender, rudbeckia, and yarrow *(Achillea)*.

Of course, these lists for drought-tolerant flowers are far from complete. I have included only those that have proved successful for me.

LEFT: *Zinnias such as the brilliant orange Torch, an All-America Selections Winner, are among my favorites for cutting. They always look beautiful in the kitchen garden, but the best news is that the more you cut for bouquets, the more they'll bloom.*

ABOVE: *Sunflowers are in full bloom against the summer sky. In case of drought, it's smart to have plants such as these that can tolerate water rationing.*

RIGHT: *Herbs such as Purple Ruffles basil are naturally heat- and drought-tolerant, especially if the soil is well-prepared and receives ample moisture during the initial weeks of growth. The idea is to get the roots established before they are stressed too much.*

The best time to harvest strawflowers such as these Bright Bikinis Mix helichrysums is when the blooms are not quite fully open; those showing yellow centers are past their prime for use as dried flowers.

RIGHT: Here I am experimenting with drying roses by the hanging method.

Drying Flowers

An amazing statistic to note is that the seed sales of flowers for drying have tripled in the last five years. Although I don't dry flowers often, I do know something about dried flowers and feel it's important to mention them, since they're so popular. The process will allow you to lengthen the pleasure you get from the flowers in your garden and also provide you with raw material for holiday decorations and gifts.

The real difference between dried and fresh flowers is simply the absence of moisture. If you intend to become knowledgeable and proficient, then you will have to spend some time learning about the changes that take place during the drying process; most flowers change in color, size, and even shape. I will give you a list of flowers that dry well, but you will need to experiment to see how the flowers of your choice turn out.

Each flower has its own requirements for growing, but the trick to drying lies in proper harvesting and post-harvesting care. Of course, some flowers dry easier and better than others. A great deal of your success in drying flowers will be affected by the humidity at harvesting and drying time. You may dry flowers in any stage of bloom from just-opened buds to mature flowers. But, remember, your flowers will open a bit as they dry; if picked at the peak of maturity, they are likely to fall apart. Experiment to find the blooming cycle that produces the color and fragrance you desire. Allow six to twelve inches of stem, if possible; the strongest center stem is usually the best. Choose a sunny, dry day and harvest your flowers as soon as the dew is off the petals, before the midday sun. Remove all heavy foliage and undesirable leaves before drying.

Hanging is a traditional and no-fuss method for drying, particularly for flowers that are everlastings, meaning those with papery parts that retain their form and color after being dried, such as strawflowers, globe amaranth, and statice. Bunch a few, no more than six stems, of the same variety. The smaller the bunches, the better and faster the flowers will dry. I wrap these together with a rubber band; this is very important, because as the stems dry, they shrink, and the rubber band will hold tight. Hang them head down in a warm, dry, dark place with good air circulation; an attic is ideal. The darkness is important, as it helps prevent fading.

The drying period differs for each type of flower and the drying conditions, and can be anywhere from three days to three weeks. Check your flowers regularly by touching them with your fingers; remove any that mildew. When they are dry and rigid, they're ready and should then be taken to a cooler place and prepared for an arrangement or stored by placing them carefully in large, corrugated cartons until you are ready to work with them.

FLOWERS FOR TRADITIONAL ATTIC DRYING— AND WHEN TO PICK

Astilbe: when the color first appears in June

Allium, including chives: before or after they go to seed in June, depending on the form you want

Yarrow: from June to August when flowers first open

Globe thistle: from June to August when blue hue first appears

Celosia: smaller side shoots in August; the earlier, larger flowers are harder to dry properly

Statice: in August when buds first open

Blue salvia: in August when buds first open

Teasel: when pods are naturally dried on the plant

Strawflower: for varieties with long, slender abundant petals, any time during the summer when only one ring of petals has opened and color is scarcely visible; for varieties with shorter petals, two rings of petals may be open. Pick flower heads only of the strawflowers, not stems. Lay the freshly picked flower heads in a single layer with space between on a screen or in a drying basket; later add a stem of green florist wire

Globe amaranth: any time during the summer when heads are still moist and full of color. The new pink and orangy ones are as pretty dried as they are in the garden

Ageratum: flower bunches that have just opened and are still deeply colored

MORE ANNUALS
THAT CAN BE DRIED UPSIDE DOWN

Baby's breath *(Gypsophila)*
Bells of Ireland *(Moluccella)*
Bee balm *(Monarda)*
Chinese lantern
Cockscomb
Dusty Miller
Everlastings of all types
Seed heads of ornamental grasses
Honesty
Larkspur (annual)
Marigold
Okra

There are several other methods for drying flowers. You can, for example, space them in an upright position on a wire-mesh screen in the same type of attic environment in which you dry hanging flowers. Calendula, zinnia, daisy, and marigold all dry well with this method; the mesh supports the flower head. Glycerol can help preserve flowers that tend to shrink after drying, such as baby's breath, which when hung to dry can shrink to one-quarter its normal size. Place the stem of baby's breath in a mixture of one-third glycerine to two-thirds water for three weeks until glycerol is felt on the flowers.

To preserve better the color and shape of flowers with fleshier and more delicate petals—such as peonies and roses (roses also dry well but differently from the traditional hanging method)—try a drying compound. A mixture of three parts' borax to one of clean sand preserves petal texture and shape better. Silica gel allows flowers to maintain vibrant colored petals after drying. Do your own experimenting and try drying your flowers with different methods. When using the borax/sand mixture or silica gel, cut flowers at the same time you would for traditional drying, but keep only a short stem—about one and a half inches. You will need a tin with an airtight cover; place about two inches of your drying mix in the bottom of the tin. Place the flowers (one kind to a tin) upright in the compound and slowly, carefully bury the blossom with more compound; use a toothpick to gently pry apart the petals for more even coverage. When dry (check in a few days), wires can be inserted carefully into the bottom of the flower head to simulate a stem. Camouflage the wire with green floral tape.

Of course, there are always those looking for the quick fix, and you can be sure one has been found in the microwave-oven drying method. Cover the flowers on a platter with silica gel. As the microwave cooks the flowers, the moisture is absorbed by the silica gel. Since microwaves vary so much, it's difficult to tell you what setting to use; however, the average cooking temperature is 160 degrees F. Cooking time is two to two and one-half minutes, and standing time is ten to thirty minutes. I've never tried this method, but anyone interested in drying different kinds of flowers will find it fun and useful to experiment with microwaving.

After you've achieved satisfactory dried flowers, use a delicate hand in creating crafts from them. Handle your dried flowers with TLC and be patient—each of your creations will be different and delicate. Experiment to see what works best for you. You may create a holiday decoration that will be in your family for years to come; it can be cleaned and refurbished annually with fresh materials, but always basically the same, your own style and tradition.

Globe amaranth Strawberry Fields is a welcome new color for this old-fashioned everlasting.

RIGHT: *Baby's breath, or gypsophila, is available in both annual and perennial forms and in white or pink, single- or double-flowered.*

LEFT: *Carefree Wonder represents a newly created class of shrub roses that are strong enough to get on in the garden with other plants and without undue fussing.*

RIGHT: *Slightly overblown roses make gorgeous bouquets.*

BELOW: *A Japanese beetle on a favorite color rose. The beetles find pale yellow and white roses nearly irresistible.*

Growing Roses

Don't shy away from roses—they're not as difficult as most people think. If you're a beginning gardener, you might try almost any potted rose you find blooming at your neighborhood garden store; let your eyes and nose tell you which one, then buy it and start to learn about how to grow roses in your own garden with your own set of growing conditions. Just remember these basic rules.

• Roses need a lot of sunlight—several hours or a half day—with room between and all around for fresh air to circulate freely.

• Roses also need a lot of water, and along with this, they require excellent drainage; never plant them where a standing pool of water can accumulate.

• Fertilize your roses in spring and then again in the middle of June with a handful of special rose fertilizer; work this into the top two inches of soil around the bushes.

• Spray once a week to control powdery mildew and blackspot; try using a tablespoon of baking soda to a gallon of water. If this doesn't seem to be working, I mix a dash of Funginex with an insecticidal soap; be sure to check labels for compatibility when mixing soaps and chemical sprays.

• I find the best method against Japanese beetles is picking by hand and crushing them or dropping them in kerosene or rubbing alcohol.

• Prune once a year in early spring when they are still dormant or just breaking dormancy; remove all thin and weak wood entirely and cut back the strong shoots by about half their length.

• In summer, don't forget to deadhead or snip off blooms when they fade.

The Vegetable Garden

In summer, the vegetable garden makes every meal an abundance of earthly delights. As I walk through my garden, I nibble on strawberries and tomatoes fresh off the vine, while I decide what vegetables I will have for dinner. Summer squash, green beans, corn, broccoli, potatoes, cauliflower, carrots, beets: it's so much fun to choose. This time of year is what we've all been waiting

LEFT: *Summer squash such as this yellow zucchini from Burpee add variety to the menu and inspire the cook to try new dishes and combinations.*

ABOVE: *Plant shell beans in prepared soil that is kept evenly moist, especially the first two or three weeks. Early bean shoots a few weeks later.*

RIGHT: *An icebox watermelon hangs in cheesecloth against a sunny wall to speed its ripening.*

A dewy bed of tender spinach, just right for picking.

RIGHT: *Sweet peppers come in the most astonishing colors. Here is a deep purple one, most dramatic in salads.*

RIGHT: *Lemon Boy Hybrid tomato produces a vigorous plant that is resistant to nematodes and verticillium and fusarium wilts. Staking helps produce blemish-free fruits.*

for. After you eat the first planting in spring, extend the growing season in your vegetable beds as long as possible by succession sowings of cool-weather, short-season crops such as spinach, beets, carrots, lettuce, and scallions. When the summer hot weather sets in, make successive sowings of crops such as beans, and at the end of August, begin sowing cool-weather crops again.

Vegetables that perform well in the high temperatures of midsummer are cucumber, muskmelon, okra, squash, tomato, eggplant, pepper, and watermelon. However, never neglect watering. If you've ever grown misshapen cucumbers with a bitter taste, you may have been guilty of holding back on the water. Cukes can take heat, but they need regular watering—about one-half inch per week when the vines are young, and one or more inches per week when the weather warms and vines elongate and fruit sets. During the hot months, wilting often occurs before mid-morning. If so, your plants need a good soaking at least six inches deep; mulching will minimize moisture loss. Also, make certain your garden soil is well supplied with the proper nutrients. If cucumbers seem bitter to you anyway, then peel them before eating—the bitterness

usually lies just beneath the skin (along with the burps). And try growing a specially hybridized, bitter-free variety, such as Marketmore 70.

Unlike cucumbers, tomatoes are more likely to be troubled by excessive watering—one of the causes of blossom-end rot, a calcium deficiency in the fruit that makes it rot from the bottom as soon as it sets. Blossom-end rot can also be caused by too much nitrogen in the soil, too close cultivation so that air can't get around between the tomatoes, or rapid plant growth followed by a dry spell. I find tomatoes do best in raised beds, especially if soil is naturally wet; good drainage is essential, and mulching with about four inches of straw will keep moisture levels even. With tomatoes, or any vegetable for that matter, avoid using high nitrogen fertilizers or too fresh manure (not under six months old).

If you're a new gardener, you may find it challenging at first to determine when some of your crops are ready to eat. Of course, tomatoes, lettuce, beans, and peas are obvious, but what about corn and melons? As cornstalks grow and mature, you will notice at the top of the stalk a tassle, which is where the pollen is. Lower down on the stalk, the husks form; off the end of the husk are the silks. The pollen from the tassle pollinates the silks. When the silks turn brown and dry, the husk becomes really tight, and milky juice squirts out if you pierce a kernel—that's when sweet corn is ready to harvest, but not before you have the kettle of water already boiling on the stove!

The silks at the end of the cornstalk during pollination. A perfect ear of sweet corn ready to harvest. How Sweet It Is Hybrid, the sweetest sweet corn this side of heaven, is served. Bon appétit!

FAR LEFT: A single perfect Peale rose.

A morning basket full of Asiatic hybrid lilies, hydrangea, achillea, verbascum, summer phlox, clematis, white physostegia, stokesia, and Goldenglow rudbeckia waiting to be moved indoors.

Here, I am deadheading a dwarf geranium to ensure continuous bloom and healthier growth. This can be beneficial therapy for the gardener as well!

RIGHT: *Tree-form lantanas, clipped globes of rosemary, large terra-cotta pots of dwarf Japanese cutleaf maples, a Gold-heart ivy topiary, and assorted geraniums are grouped on my terrace steps.*

Now, a melon is a little more difficult. First determine when it looks ripe; then, if you have patience, weigh it daily on some old bathroom scale—when no weight gain occurs for three days, it's ready to eat.

With all the fresh produce from your prolific vegetable garden, you will find yourself eating more vegetables than ever—and cooking them, too. If you've ever cooked bunches of broccoli, cauliflower, cabbage, or other cole crops, you're familiar with the unpleasant odor these vitamin-rich vegetables often produce. Let me pass along a little secret—simply adding 2 four-inch-long pieces of celery to the cooking pot eliminates that odor.

Patio Gardening

There is something so appealing about a mass of flowers overflowing from pots or spilling out of hanging containers. Virtually any container will do, so long as it has a hole in the bottom for drainage and room for enough soil medium so that the plant roots will not be cramped. The larger the container, the less often you will have to water.

Annuals are perfect for tubs, pots, and planters on patios; they are ideal for window boxes, too. You can start your own annuals from seed or buy them full-grown from your local garden center. In a sunny loca-

Mandevilla sanderi *Red Riding Hood blooms nonstop for me; I have it trained both as a large wreath and on a tepee or tripod built from four-foot bamboo stakes.*

Finding a blue passionflower in bloom is a thrilling experience no matter how often or how many. I train the vines on trellis obelisks painted dark green. They spend winters in my sun-heated pit greenhouse.

Lantana camara, *or yellow sage, blooms profusely in hot weather and full sun. I like to train these into tree-form standards about four feet tall; two of mine are nearly twenty years old. The same species comes in several colors, including creamy white and pale yellow. The aromatic leaves are sometimes used as herbal tea, hence "yellow sage."*

Creeping thyme makes a wonderful groundcover for large patio pots—seen here under one of my Japanese cutleaf maples—and between the bricks or other pavers of a terrace.

RIGHT: Ixora coccinea, or *flame-of-the-woods*, blooms with unbelievable profusion all summer. I have the bush in a ten-inch pot that stands on the steps of a green trellis pavilion overlooking the tennis court. This plant is acid loving and appreciates regular fertilizing with 30-10-10 (Miracid).

tion, they'll provide a colorful display all summer long; some of the easiest flowers to grow in containers are geraniums, marigolds, petunias, and nasturtiums. Pansies are ideal for spring displays and chrysanthemums for late summer into fall. Deadheading will ensure continuous bloom—pinch off the old blossoms as they wither.

If your containers are not in full sun, don't worry. Some of the flowers that are my favorites for hanging pots prefer filtered sunlight. Morning sun is fine, but direct afternoon sun can burn tender leaves of impatiens and fuchsias. Petunias and hanging geraniums, able to take more direct sun, also look striking in hanging containers. All containers, but particularly hanging pots that are exposed on all sides to heat and breezes, require regular watering, often every day. Because the constant watering robs the soil medium of necessary nutrients, feed the plants with a liquid fertilizer nearly every week.

Another way to dress up a brick patio is with moss or creeping thyme. Both can be established if there is just a bit of soil between the bricks; moss grows in shady locations in acidic soil, while thyme prefers sun and a higher pH. Try transplanting moss between bricks; you can purchase it, or perhaps it already grows in a moist part of your garden. Keep

newly transplanted moss moist with plain water or a weak manure tea (wrap well-rotted manure in cheese-cloth and soak in water for twenty-four hours; dilute in water and apply so that it is the color of weak tea). It is best to scatter seed for spreading thyme *(Thymus praecox arcticus)* in early fall for spring germination. Pull out any weeds by hand; never use a weed killer.

Summering Indoor Plants

A vacation outdoors can perk up many of your house-plants. Wait until the weather is consistently warm, especially at night, before bringing them out. Some will thrive in full sun; but others such as aloe, which happily takes all the sun you can give it indoors in winter, can be burned and develop unsightly spots in all-day sun outdoors. Introduce even sun lovers to full sun gradually, moving from shade to light shade before direct sun. And always bring your plants back indoors a few weeks before the heat is turned on in your house. Check to be sure there are no unwanted insect pests before crossing the threshold; a good strong spray of water should remove any. And, if a serious infestation is discovered, knock off as many as you can with water, then after the plants have drained and dried a little, spray them thoroughly with insecticidal soap.

LEFT: *Brunfelsia is called yesterday, today, and tomorrow because the flowers open a dark purple-blue and fade to nearly white by the third day. They give off a light, lemony scent and grow on a small shrub that makes an excellent patio plant.*

Goldheart English ivy may tolerate relatively low light indoors, but it really prefers full sun outdoors. I have mine trained on a pineapple-shaped metal topiary form with lemon thyme as a groundcover. The bench painted dark green was designed by the late Sir Edwin Lutyens, an English architect who worked with the English gardenmaker Gertrude Jekyll.

A garden of yew topiaries was Russell Page's idea. Here is how it looked in the early stages, about ten years before the next photograph was taken and five years before the one in winter (page 43). My gardening pal Elvin McDonald is the topiaries' official hairdresser. He uses hand-held hedge clippers, stands on a very tall ladder, and encourages the topiaries to be "nice and fluffy" at Russell's direction.

RIGHT: *These five whimsical topiary yew trees were placed here several years ago at the suggestion of my gardening pal Russell Page.*

The Templeton Garden

The beauty of my summer garden always reminds me of my dear gardening pal Russell Page. Sadly, he's no longer on this earth. I always adored having him visit us on weekends, and he was a tremendous inspiration in the planning and development of my garden.

I met Russell Page years ago outside Paris at the Moulin des Tuilleries, the country property of the Duke and Duchess of Windsor. Russell was a marvelously imposing giant of a man, and being with him on a social basis, I always found him to be charming and fun. Many people say Russell was a snob, and I can't disagree. But, on the other hand, I don't see anything wrong with that; I think being a snob means being choosy about the people you want to be with and not caring about the people you don't choose. Russell was certainly like that. For that matter, so am I.

I remember Russell and the Duke of Windsor being up early and out in the Moulin gardens for several hours every morning. They had great fun gardening together. I don't know what they talked about, but years later Russell told me that those mornings with His Royal Highness were some of the happiest times of his life. Russell often accompanied His Royal Highness to Windsor Castle to see what new, rare plants were available. The Duke of Windsor was very knowledgeable in his own right, and together he and Russell would select flowers and plants they felt would enhance the gardens of the Moulin. During these visits to Windsor Castle, Russell was impressed that upon entering the sovereign's gate, His Royal Highness would always stop to speak with the guards for at least fifteen minutes. Russell said the Duke of Windsor was obviously a very well-loved man.

Russell and I didn't really start gardening together until some years after the death of the Duke of Windsor. Russell had created gardens for many of my friends in Europe and in the United States. Every time he came to New York, he would call and spend the weekend with Winston (my late husband) and me at our property in Old Westbury. And he'd say "C. Z., when are you and I going to do a garden together?" But at that time, I already had what I considered to be an adequate kitchen garden; and I was more interested in my horses, fox hunting, horse shows, and racing than in expanding my gardens. Russell kept after me, though, and one day I just said, "What the heck! Let's see what you can do!" We walked around the property for hours, and his ideas came bubbling forth like an erupting volcano. "We'll redesign the rosebeds. And here, in this nook between the kitchen garden and the formal rose garden, we'll create a topiary garden, and here by the pool, we'll plant pond lilies. We'll reorganize the kitchen garden in sections . . ." and on and on and on.

I suppose the reason I enjoyed working with Russell so much was that we saw eye-to-eye on almost everything. He was a most sophisticated gardener but in a simple way. He knew all about plants and plant care from the most exotic lily to common lawn grass,

and he taught me what to plant, where and how to take care of it. He taught me how to make a well-organized, beautiful yet functional garden. As I said, Russell Page was a tremendous inspiration to me, and because of his influence and the skills he taught me, I've been able to create here on my property in Old Westbury truly a paradise.

Templeton House in Summer

June, July, and August are when my garden is vibrant with color, and I bring this beauty indoors. Throughout my house, vases overflow with flowers fresh from the garden: Gloriosa daisies, Shasta daisies, cosmos, lilies galore, and all varieties of sunflowers.

They offer a delightful contrast to my potted orchids. Early in the summer, there may be pots of the orange-red haemanthus, or blood lily, with ball-shaped heads of flowers that remind me of fireworks going off. At about the same time, we often bring in some of the cut heads of the giant ornamental onion, *Allium giganteum*. Later, there will be four or five different colors and types of annual sunflowers, which always make me smile when I see them, and in some rare, green ceramic frogs I like to mass bunches of very short-stemmed marigolds in my favorite shade of orange.

Sunflowers always make me smile when I see them. Here, they are arranged with fresh-cut dill in a green, plastic pail. The blue, plastic watering can is the kind I favor because it is lightweight and won't rust.

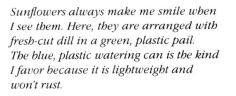

LEFT: Symphonie popcorn comes in several beautiful colors and mixtures. The dried ears become decorations at Halloween and Thanksgiving.

This photo captures the beauty of my garden in full summer. Healthy soil has boosted my How Sweet It Is Hybrid sweet corn at least as high as an elephant's eye!

A glowing selection of fancy gourds light the house with bright colors.

4 Fall

Fall is probably the busiest season of all. Even as you continue to harvest your late-summer vegetables, such as corn, beets, carrots, onions, horseradish, string beans, and chard, you must start thinking about cleanup for winter and preparation for next year.

This season is also an ideal time to plant trees and shrubs. Most newly planted woody ornamentals have a better survival rate if planted in fall rather than spring. This is due to the better soil and air temperatures and, it is hoped, ample rainfall at that time of year, all of which aid in establishing a proper root system, so long as you plant at least a few weeks before the first frost.

And, if you want flowers in bloom in late winter and early next spring, now is the time to decide what bulbs you want and to put them in the ground. Plant spring-flowering bulbs after the cool weather sets in but before the frost hits your area so that the soil is still workable. The first bulbs to flower, even as early as February on Long Island, are snowdrops and crocuses, then hyacinths, grape hyacinths, and daffodils. Species tulips begin to bloom in March or early April, then single and double early tulips followed by midseason tulips: Darwin hybrid, triumph, Mendel, and *Tulipa greigii*. The beautiful late tulips—Darwin, cottage, parrot, lily-flowered, and fringed—reach their peaks in May and are especially colorful for cutting.

When you're thinking about bulbs for next spring, you are following my number one rule, *plan ahead.* Now, remember the title of this book, *5 Seasons of Gardening,* and think not only of spring but of the springtime holidays also. And, if you're planning to have flowering bulbs for the fall holidays, you must begin preparations even earlier—by the first of October. (For information on forcing bulbs, see chapter 5, "Holidays.")

Spring-flowering bulbs are planted just before the ground freezes in your area; many summer flowers growing from bulbs, corms, rhizomes, and tubers require the milder temperatures of spring planting. The following chart lists some of my favorites, the best planting season for each, and the proper depth for planting. To most of us, a bulb is a bulb, but technical differences exist that divide plants having these underground storage systems into bulbs, tubers, corms, and rhizomes. No matter what they are or what we call them, most need a half day or more of direct sunshine in order to grow and bloom well and manufacture through the maturing leaves the energy needed for the next season's growth and flowering.

Peppers sweet and hot come in many colors and shapes. We start the seeds in a warm growing house about eight weeks before planting-out weather, around Memorial Day, and the harvest begins in earnest after July Fourth.

My dog Tiger and I are out gathering summer squash, a warm-weather plant that comes to a grinding halt after fall's first cold snap.

You can harvest fresh horseradish root in the fall, after the leaves have finished their season's work of gathering energy. Notice the hose: I like to keep all my garden hoses neatly coiled and racked when they are not in use. This saves time in the long run and helps keep the garden looking tidy.

Planting paper-whites is an annual ritual for me. I am reminded to plant them by the sight and sounds of geese as they fly overhead on their way south. You can grow narcissi like these in bowls with pebbles and water or pot them as I am doing in plastic bulb pans filled with commercial potting soil such as Pro-Mix.

Planting Chart for My Favorite Flowers

NAME	WHEN TO PLANT	PLANTING DEPTH (INCHES)
Anemone blanda (rhizome)	plant now	3
Begonia, tuberous	wait until spring	2
Bleeding heart (rhizome)	plant now	3
Calla lily (rhizome)	wait until spring	4
Canna (rhizome)	wait until spring	6
Crocus (corm)	plant now	3
Daffodil (bulb)	plant now	8
Dahlia (tuber)	wait until spring	7
Freesia (corm)	pot up now	2
Gladiolus (corm)	wait until spring	4
Grape hyacinth (bulb)	plant now	4-5
Hyacinth (bulb)	plant now	6-8
Iris, Dutch (bulb)	plant now	4-6
Iris reticulata (bulb)	plant now	4-6
Lily—*Lilium* (bulb)	plant now	4-6
Lily of the valley (rhizome)	plant now	1-2
Narcissus (bulb)	pot up now	2
Peony (herbaceous)	plant now	1-2
Ranunculus (tuber)	pot up now	1-2
Tuberose (tuber)	wait until spring	4
Tulip (bulb)	plant now	6-8

ABOVE LEFT: *Dahlias such as this Orange Flame, large, informal, and decorative, grow from tubers that must be planted every spring and lifted in the fall before the ground freezes. They are stored through winter in a warm, dry basement.*

FAR LEFT: *Bulbs of giant Dutch hyacinth Delft Blue are planted in rows in raised beds in the kitchen garden. As they come into bloom, we dig and pot them for display in the house.*

BELOW LEFT: *Tulips such as this red-and-white parrot are planted in the kitchen garden in the fall up until the ground freezes. They give me an abundance of cut flowers all through spring.*

ABOVE: *There is a haunting beauty in the fall light when the lindens in the allée start to drop their leaves. The trees were planted in 1906 by my late husband's uncle, John S. Phipps. This is the best place on the property to really make a horse gallop.*

Here is the far end of my kitchen garden in early fall, with a white butterfly bush, or buddleia, standing at least twelve feet tall; the rosy plumes of ornamental grasses; and rows of Montauk daisies about to burst into bloom. The green trellis moon gate and fence beyond were designed by William C. Mulligan, built at Templeton, and used originally for my exhibit at the New York Flower Show.

RIGHT: *Beyond the bed of cauliflower, golden coreopsis Early Sunrise blooms abundantly. This coreopsis blooms the first year from seed, like an annual, but returns year after year thereafter as a hardy perennial.*

Perennials

Easy care, reliable, year-after-year performance is spelled very simply: perennial. Large or small, perennial beds and borders form the backbone of any flower garden by offering an array of plants to suit any taste or setting. Planted this fall, perennials will burst into bloom next spring or summer to add charm, beauty, and easy color to your garden. Perennials are perfectly suited for today's life-styles, even for those living in the "fast lane"! Most perennials multiply, so you'll have a never-ending number of new plants every few years in your garden.

As we already discussed in winter, you must have a garden plan. Your perennials are here to stay, so before you plant, plan out on paper what will give you continuous bloom, pleasing color combinations, and a variety of height, shapes, and textures.

Decide where you want your perennial garden—in shade or sun? Most perennials need sun to thrive; however, there are some shade lovers.

List your favorite perennials with their color, height, and time of flowering.

Choose plants with different bloom times, since proper planning can give you continuous flowers from spring to fall.

Here, I am dividing and replanting a division from a large clump of Siberian iris. Notice how the soil is more easily worked in the fall when it is warm and moist rather than cold and wet, which it tends to be in the spring.

FAR RIGHT: *After frost, cut herbaceous peony tops to about 4 or 5 inches from the ground. Notice we have lightly top-dressed over the center of each clump with wood ashes from the fireplace, the alkalinity of which offsets the acidity of the pine needle mulch that will be applied as soon as the ground freezes.*

Make a sketch of the garden, draw shapes to represent each plant, and write in the plant names. Of course, the taller varieties should be placed at the back and the shorter ones in front. Perennials look their best in clumps of two, three, or four of the same variety; remember, ample room for them to grow and spread is a must!

Golden coreopsis and rudbeckia will give you color all summer. For height, a mixture of hollyhocks, delphiniums, or lupines might be the answer. For shady spots, nothing beats the fluffy astilbe or the interesting foliage of the hosta. Dwarf flower varieties are ideal for small areas.

In late May or early June, my perennial gardens come alive with peonies, irises, lupines, phlox, colum-bines, coralbells, astilbes, oriental poppies, sweet Williams, and wild geraniums. My lilies, daylilies, del-phiniums, Shasta daisies, and summer phlox bloom in July, August, and September. Chrysanthemums and asters will continue until frost.

If you have already-established perennials and you feel that they're getting too big, now is the time to divide most—after they have finished blooming. Dividing huge clumps can help control disease and insect infestations. For example, overgrown clumps of bearded iris may harbor soft rot (decay) and debris

where borer moths can lay eggs. Cut back the leaves to about three inches and dig up the clump with a spade or fork. Clean away soil with a spray of water and, with a sharp knife, cut sections off the central rhizome that have at least one eye or bud and roots. Remove and discard any soft parts or any with the tiny, wormlike iris borer larvae. Then replant clumps. For best effect, each clump of iris should contain no more than three to five rhizomes. And, if you have extras, what a great gift!

Divide overgrown clumps of Siberian or Japanese iris by digging each clump out of its place in the bed, then pushing two spading forks, back to back, into the center of the crown; separate the roots by forcing the handles apart. Clean out any dead sections before replanting your new plants.

As for peonies, one of my favorites, I dig around and under the plants so as not to break off the roots. I wash the soil off with a gentle spray from the garden hose and cut off any remaining foliage. With a sharp, sterile knife, cut the roots into sections containing three to five "eyes," or red buds that appear on the roots in fall. Be sure each section has a strong root system. As you make the cuts, check for signs of disease, such as unnaturally brown or soft parts; if any are discovered, cut them away, being sure to dip your knife or clippers

in rubbing alcohol between each cut. Replant the newly divided roots immediately in a sunny or partially shaded location. And remember, set them from one to two inches deep—if you plant too deep, your peonies will not bloom; however, if they are too shallow, you risk having the roots heaved out during the freezes and thaws of winter. On Long Island, September and October are the best months for dividing peonies, to give them ample time to become established before the killing frost.

In addition to perennials, the so-called tender perennials require attention in fall. Dig up tender tubers, corms, and bulbs, such as gladiolus, tuberous begonias, and tuberoses, and store for winter before the frost hits in your area; however, others such as dahlias and cannas, needn't be dug until frost has blackened the leaves and they have been cut back to about six inches.

Be very careful when lifting these beauties, to avoid bruising. Allow them to dry well before storing; most tubers take about two weeks to "cure." Store in sand at 40 to 50 degrees F (4 to 10 degrees C), and check occasionally during the winter to make sure they don't dry out to the point of complete desiccation. Unfortunately, once out of the ground, most tubers

and bulbs look pretty much like any others, making identification of variety and color difficult. Here's how I get around this dilemma. I label my plants during their summer flowering, and then it's easy to transfer the name or color of the variety directly onto the tuber or bulb in fall using a felt-tip pen. So, come spring, it's a cinch to plant the right dahlia in the right spot.

When you find that just-right geranium flower color, you can keep it year to year. Simply take cuttings in fall and snap off stems that are four to six inches long, stripping each stem of all but three to four of the top leaves. Exposing the stems to air (in the shade) for a day will cause them to form calluses at the cut ends, which will help prevent rot. You can also dip the callused cuttings in rooting powder (available at most nurseries or garden supply stores). Set each stem in a pot filled with moist, lightly packed sterilized soil or specially prepared soil-less medium. Keep the medium moist but never soggy. After roots develop, place the pot in a bright, sunny window and let the soil dry out a little at the surface between waterings. Fertilize when new growth appears. To encourage branching, pinch back the stem tips when the plants are five inches tall. Under the proper growing conditions, the plants will start to flower in about four to five months.

LEFT: *Tender bulbs such as amaryllis must be brought inside before frost. Amaryllis pots are stored on their sides under the benches of a growing greenhouse. Only after they are completely dry is it time to remove the leaves. After eight to twelve weeks, or when flower buds appear, the pots are uprighted on the benches, and watering is resumed.*

RIGHT: *There is nothing like an organized, well-lighted potting bench to get me in the mood for some serious potting, repotting, and plant propagation. I like to have a supply of different pots, potting-mix ingredients, stakes, and ties, with an ash can to catch all the dead leaves and old soil that will be carried off to the compost pile.*

Cheyenne dahlia is a large-flowered type having quilled petals that are feathered at the tips in an unusual way. The color has a glow-in-the-dark quality that is guaranteed to cheer up the most dismal of fall days.

Despite the fact that we use no poisonous sprays, the espaliers that grow in my kitchen garden against a south-facing wall of the house produce a large crop of apples and pears.

Vegetables

With renewed interest in kitchen gardens, many gardeners find their harvests of vegetables and fruits too numerous for immediate use. Proper storage of homegrown vegetables is most important. Here are a few rules that I observe to ensure my crops store well.

Vegetables and fruits must be mature or nearly so at harvest to store well.

They must be free of all visible evidence of disease.

They should be free of severe insect damage.

Handle them carefully so that they do not become bruised or cut. Damaging makes fruits and vegetables more susceptible to mold and decay.

Harvest prior to any severe or killing frost because most fruits and vegetables do not store well if subjected to severe chilling, even if damage is not immediately visible.

It is not advisable to store vegetables and fruits together for long periods of time. Many fruits, including pears and apples, give off a gas known as ethylene, which will affect most vegetables by rapidly ripening them. On the other hand, pears and apples will absorb the flavors and odors of some vegetables.

The First Frost

The end of the season always seems to come in my garden just when the tomatoes are most productive. When the weather report forecasts a mild frost, I take action. I use a "thermo" cover, an easy-to-manage product, which is more like a fabric that keeps crops warm during light frosts and cool nights. It is installed in minutes.

The trick in using protective coverings is to fasten them properly around the plants to keep out the cold night air. Then, in the morning, remove the cover as soon as the temperature rises above 50 degrees F (10 degrees C). If frost is forecast again for that night, back goes the cover in the late afternoon.

Tomatoes aren't the only crop you will want to consider covering. By protecting other tender varieties, such as zucchini, cantaloupes, eggplants, and peppers, I can extend my delicious harvest for another week or two instead of pulling up and wasting plants ruined by the first "nip" of frost.

Although vegetables come to mind first (after all, we all love to eat!), don't forget to protect tender flowers and plants, too. Have you some fabulous dahlias just approaching their full beauty? Don't let the first frost be a "killjoy." Cover your dahlias the same way you do tomatoes. And try stretching the productivity of marigolds, zinnias, and other flowers for extended fall enjoyment by covering them, too, for a night or two when the mercury first dips. Often, an early light frost is followed by several days or weeks of warm, frost-free weather. This is the true Indian summer, and if you have chosen well what to protect from an early deep chill, big rewards of flowers and edibles will be yours.

But, when the forecast is for prolonged freezing weather, the best thing to do is pick as many flowers and vegetables as you can. Harvest those large green tomatoes as well and spread them indoors in a single layer in a box or basket to ripen in an airy place (temperature range 55 to 60 degrees F; 12 to 15 degrees C).

Garden Cleanup

Although you've kept your garden neat and tidy all summer long, the real cleanup begins when the mercury dips, and you approach winter. After you've plucked the garden's last carrot and planted that final bulb, it's time to cut back your perennials, already dying back, remove entirely the remains of all the annuals, and rake up the debris. It's very important to rake up *every* particle of debris so no hiding place is left for unwanted bugs. A clean garden is a healthy one.

Today, with closed and closing landfills, it makes good environmental sense to recycle as much of this garden debris as you possibly can. Recycle it all—except for diseased and insect-infested plants and those pesky weeds that you can't seem to get rid of. I strongly suggest investing in a lightweight, inexpensive electric shredder. It will help you reduce your debris to one-eighth the original volume—in other words, what used to fill eight bags now fits into one. This shredded material, often referred to as humus, is compact and can be composted or used as mulch. A four- to six-inch layer of shredded leaves and grass clippings will protect tender plants over the winter and help preserve moisture, reducing the need to water.

Take a lesson from nature. Consider the forest; in fall, deciduous trees drop their leaves as they prepare for winter dormancy. The leaves accumulate at the base of each tree and create layer upon layer as the years sail by. Nature is building up a mulch—which fertilizes and enriches the soil—beneath every tree. Earthworms, beneficial insects, and friendly bacteria immediately set to work breaking down the leaves on the forest floor. We all dread raking leaves—"nature's jewels"—but the labor is not in vain if we save the leaves and use them in our gardens. Replenishing your soil with leaves, as the forest does, will improve your soil structure and fertility; your garden will burst with energy.

Leaf mulch is excellent for evergreens, especially shallow-rooted rhododendrons and azaleas. Use it also for roses and on bulb beds, to prevent alternate freezing and thawing. As leaf mulch decomposes and improves the soil, it also lowers the pH, making the soil more acidic, which is usually fine for acid-loving rhododendrons and azaleas. But, for roses and bulbs, you will most likely have to balance the increased acidity by adding a little garden lime, which raises the pH; be sure to have your soil tested every few years to maintain the desired pH.

Fall is also the time we rototill the kitchen garden beds and top-dress all over with at least a two-inch layer of rotted horse manure. I always put a blanket of pine needles and oak leaves over my perennials because I just don't like seeing them in the winter without covers on!

Tool Cleanup

As you put your garden to bed for the winter—cleaned up and covered up—it is important that you do the same for your equipment. Inspect, clean, and treat all your hand tools; winterize power tools; and store chemicals in a dark, frost-free place, also safely away from stoves, furnaces, and high temperatures. Wire brush and sharpen all tools with cutting edges. Some—such as shovels, spades, hoes, and trowels—will need just a metal file to crisp up the edges; others, such as pruning clippers and saws, hedge trimmers and lawn mowers, require a Carborundum stone or even professional sharpening. Lightly oil the cutting edges along with any moving parts to prevent rust. Check handles and stress points for cracks and weakness. Replace any unsatisfactory parts.

Power lawn mowers and rototillers require special care. After sharpening the blades, remove the spark plug and clean or replace. Ditto for the air filter and oil filter, if so equipped. Run the engine until the oil is hot, then drain and replace. For riding mowers, oil movable parts on the mower deck and check belts for tightness and wear.

In northern states, drain the fuel tank and run the engine until it stops. Take out the spark plug and clean or replace after squirting a tablespoon of oil into the cylinder head to prevent rust. Pull the starter rope once monthly.

Remove the battery from riding mowers; recharge if necessary and store on wood (never cement), in a

The kitchen garden beds are top-dressed with rotted horse manure and mulched.

Cold, rainy days are a good time to soak, wash, sort, and store all pots and other empty containers. Soaking several hours or overnight in a solution made at the rate of a cup of cider vinegar to each gallon of water will soften mineral deposits that are otherwise stubborn to remove from the walls and rims of clay pots.

Late fall is when you'll be happiest to have
a greenhouse, whatever the size. I try
to inspect each plant carefully, remove
all dead leaves, prune if necessary, and
get rid of any and all bugs by spraying
with insecticidal soap.

cool, dry place. Wire brush battery terminals and coat with a thin layer of grease.

Finally, inspect all your containers of horticultural oil, insecticidal soap, and other toxic chemicals for leaks and loose-fitting caps. Store in a cool, dry place (do not freeze), where there is proper ventilation and they will be out of reach of "tiny hands" and pets.

Early Fall Gardening Calendar

Early fall before the ground freezes is one of the best times to fertilize shrubs and trees. Nutrients are still taken up by the roots and transmitted to the plants in early spring, but use only a low-nitrogen fertilizer at this time; a 0-6-5 or 1-6-5 fertilizer will help harden the wood, making it more cold-hardy and enhancing next spring's flower crop.

Deciduous trees and conifer evergreens can still be planted throughout the month of November on Long Island. Remember to water all new trees and shrubs and even established ones during periods of drought; it is especially important that trees and shrubs go into winter freeze-up with an adequate supply of moisture throughout the root zones.

Add a complete fertilizer, organic matter, and garden lime (if soil pH requires it) to areas where only vegetables and annuals have been growing. It is best to plow or spade this into the earth.

Before the ground freezes drive in stakes around newly planted evergreens for windbreaks; water, mulch with leaves, and then later in December, create windbreaks by attaching polyethylene or burlap to the stakes.

Heavily mulch broad-leaved evergreens, boxwood, and other surface-rooted shrubs before the ground freezes to minimize winter damage. If these grow in exposed areas, use burlap windbreaks to protect from the sun and desiccating winds.

Protect your rosebushes by hilling up with ten to

twelve inches of soil over the base of the plant—the perfect winter protection for the crown.

Cover strawberry beds with four to six inches of straw or salt hay and add a heavy mulch around the root zones of raspberries.

Saturate gypsy moth egg cases—found on fences, tree trunks, and logs—with creosote, now and throughout the winter.

Winter Forecasting

For centuries, farmers have predicted winter by garden folklore, and the farmers who knew the most proverbs about weather were also the most prepared for the oncoming difficulties. I've found that most sayings stand a good chance of being correct for short-range forecasting.

Here are a few folk adages that I watch for each season:

• *If the cock molts before the hen, we'll have winter thick and thin; if the hen molts before the cock, we'll have winter hard as rock.*

• *If squirrels have extra fur and very bushy tails, it will be a cold winter.*

• *If squirrels bury their nuts close to the surface of the ground, it will be a harsh winter.*

• *If oak leaves stay on trees into December, it will be a mild winter.*

• *If a chipmunk is seen in December, it will be a mild winter.*

• *If the woolly caterpillar has a broad band, then it will be a warm winter; thin band, then a cold winter.*

• *If skunks are exceptionally fat, it will be a hard winter.*

• *If the feathers are far down on grouses' legs, it will be a tough winter.*

• *If the webs of a partridge's feet are bigger than usual, there will be a lot of snow.*

• *If a dog's winter coat is thicker than normal, it will be a tough winter.*

• *Onion skin very thin, mild winter coming in. Onion skin thick and rough, winter's going to be real tough!*

Here's another bit of folk wisdom to help you year round. Learn to tell the temperature by listening to the crickets. Just count the number of chirps in fifteen seconds, add forty to this figure, and you have the current temperature.

Indoor Gardening

Now is the time when you'll be so happy to have your greenhouse, whatever the size. It's time to move tender potted plants indoors—jasmines, lantanas, orchids, and geraniums. Inspect them carefully and remove all dead leaves, prune vigorously and get rid of any and all bugs. I take care of these with an insecticidal soap spray.

Looking Back

Let me say again and again, if you're well-organized and you've planned ahead, this will all be easy. If you're a new gardener, and you've made some mistakes this year, learn from them. Write down what worked and what didn't. And change your system, if necessary, to make things work better for you next year.

We're approaching winter—the quiet time for thinking and planning. I always vow to make a bigger, even better garden next year.

In the larger greenhouse are a variety of cattleyas and a miniature cymbidium mixed with flowering holiday cacti, ready to be put on display in the house; vanda orchids grow in the background.

For Christmas dinner in the main dining room, we'll get out the cranberry glass and bring in pots of red amaryllis and poinsettias.

Holidays

The holidays, and the frost is on the pumpkin! I love this time of year, when my head is full of thoughts of decorating my house and table.

First, Halloween!

Of course, pumpkins are at the head of everyone's list for this festive holiday. If you're a pumpkin lover, as I am, then you planted yours in the spring, and by now you have great orange beauties. Don't forget to plant fancy gourds as well: they come in just about every shape, size, and color.

I find pumpkins attractive carved into jack-o'-lanterns or uncarved, just sitting on the porch or next to the front door in a variety of sizes and shapes. For your Halloween dinner table, have you ever hollowed out a pumpkin, put a candle inside, and used it as the centerpiece? Depending on the size of your table, the centerpiece can be especially attractive with small gourds or even berries arranged around the pumpkin.

Although your garden is probably finished by now, Mother Nature is still quite a provider at this time of year; so let your imagination run wild. Take a walk into the woods or fields with a pair of clippers and see what you can find! Even neatly tied stacks of dried cornstalks can make a wonderful statement at your entrance or doorway. And, the best part about all of these Halloween decorations is that they will still look great when Thanksgiving arrives!

You can keep those colorful, decorative gourds beautiful all winter long. After you pick them, let them dry first and then coat your favorites with a clear acrylic spray or varnish. For an added touch of fall beauty, make an arrangement by surrounding your gourds with a few colorful autumn leaves.

Then Comes Thanksgiving

At Thanksgiving, I always like to decorate my house using the traditional fall colors: bronzes, golds, yellows, oranges, and burgundy reds. The very best flower for this holiday is the chrysanthemum, which is still blooming on Long Island in November and comes in just about any color of the rainbow. You can have chrysanthemums as cut flowers in vases or as potted plants. To have really abundant, bushy chrysanthemums, you have to plan ahead! Begin in the spring, when plants are six to eight inches tall, and pinch back the main stem to two or three leaves. Vigorous growth appears above each leaf stem, and this growth is also pinched back when it reaches six to eight inches. Keep pinching until the middle of July, and you'll have a bushy plant by fall.

In addition to mums, for a little variety I sometimes have gloxinias, sedums, or kalanchoes. Kalanchoes are especially easy to have in bloom and in all sizes, from tiny thumb pots that delight any very small visitors to twelve-inch shallow bulb pans that may have

hundreds of bright flowers open all at once. Make tip cuttings of kalanchoe any time in the summer. Stick them an inch deep in moist, clean potting soil, and they will be rooted and growing enthusiastically on their own in a couple of weeks. Kalanchoes come in bright reds and pinks, but also in burnished oranges and apricots, which I happen to favor. Generally, for Thanksgiving and through the end of November, my feeling is autumn: warm colors, dried arrangements, pumpkins, gourds, and corn.

I do make at least one exception to the usual fall colors, and that is to have lots of pots of the Mexican tuberose, some single-flowered, others double. It takes

only one spike of these to perfume a large room, but at this festive season of giving thanks, I like to have many pots. I've never known anyone else to do this with tuberoses, but I pot up each clump of tubers in spring or early summer in a ten-inch, green, plastic azalea pot. I set the pots in rows outdoors near one of the greenhouses and give them lots of water and fertilizer throughout the summer. By early autumn, blooms are coming up from every clump of grassy leaves. These last for several weeks when brought into the house. After the flowers finish blooming, the pots are turned on their sides under a bench in the greenhouse, or sometimes in the basement of my house, and the

LEFT: *An abundant crop of pumpkins harvested just in time for Halloween.*

RIGHT: *Here, I have placed a hardy orange mum in a pot next to the similarly colored wall of my front hall.*

BELOW: *The library is never more festive or inviting than at Thanksgiving, when we bring in woven baskets of hardy chrysanthemums in the traditional fall colors: bronzes, golds, yellows, oranges.*

tubers are left to rest in the soil until repotting time the following season.

The Christmas Holiday

After Thanksgiving, the decorative mood changes. The geese are honking their way south, and the cold air hints of snow—winter is here. I change the color scheme in my house from fall bronzes and golds to festive red and white as well as Christmas greenery. Christmas flowers for me include poinsettias, amaryllis, lilies of the valley, orchids, and a small army of paper-white narcissi.

Precooled bulbs of paper-white narcissus and amaryllis take from about four to ten weeks to flower from potting up, depending on the variety. The simplest method for forcing these is to use Pro-mix, a commercially prepared soil-less medium comprised of sphagnum peat moss, perlite, vermiculite, and other goodies; it's clean and convenient and seems to nurture healthy roots and tops. If you stagger bulb plantings every week or so, you'll have them continually through the holiday season, for Thanksgiving, Christmas, and New Year's.

I decorate my house in the old traditional Christmas way. The reason is simple: each piece of

LEFT: *In the growing greenhouse, a bench of kalanchoes in small pots is ready to be taken into the house. These cheerful plants are extremely easy to grow, stay in bloom for several weeks, and since they are succulents, won't go to pieces the first time someone forgets to water.*

BELOW: *In addition to mums, for a little variety at almost any holiday, I sometimes have gloxinias like this red-and-white polka-dot variety.*

RIGHT: *All through the fall holidays, I have pots of the Mexican tuberose, both double like this one and single-flowered.*

LEFT: *A festive grouping of red and white amaryllis and paper-whites. Although all paper-whites look about the same, some varieties, such as Ziva, bloom much earlier than others.*

ABOVE: *Late fall is an ideal time to prune evergreens such as these pines that surround Templeton. We always save the best for wiring into Christmas roping to festoon the front hall and stair banister and to make big wreaths for every door.*

I always have a centerpiece for my Christmas dining table that is made of evergreen clippings from around the property—pine, balsam, and holly—with fat, red candles set to flicker warmly as my family and guests arrive.

I have a very large species camellia with single red flowers that makes a perfect Christmas decoration when it is placed in the front hall inside an enormous white K'ang-hsi cachepot. The elephant tusks are from an African elephant Winston shot in 1938. This was long before anyone realized how abused and endangered elephants would become.

A close-up of one of the flowers on the camellia.

Christmas greenery has its own special meaning, the origins dating back in history thousands of years.

I start my Christmas decorating by placing a big wreath of balsam fir, which doesn't shed, on the front door, which is itself painted a lovely shade of sage blue-green. The making of wreaths dates back to ancient Greece, where they were worn by brides as symbols of good luck and happiness. The circular shape, having neither beginning nor end, symbolizes eternity. The pinecones on a wreath were used by guardian spirits of Babylon for the daily ritual of sprinkling the tree of life, to keep demons from attacking. The scent of the pine wreath was believed to drive away evil spirits from the house at Christmastime.

Holly is another good luck piece of Christmas greenery. The ancient Romans thought it had the ability to ward off lightning, evil spells, and poisonous vapors. If a holly tree grows in your garden, you have another piece of good fortune. Pruning of fruiting hollies is best done just before Christmas, and why not use the short branches for your own decorations? All other pruning at this time should be limited to taking out diseased or dead wood and crossed branches. (Trimming to make the trees compact in habit or dense can also be done during early spring before growth starts.) And by the way, on a more modern note, George Washington was a famous horticulturist who appreciated holly. He recorded in his diary that in the early part of the year 1785, he spent several days planting holly trees at Mt. Vernon. His set of false teeth were reported to have been made of the white, hard-grained holly wood.

Every Christmas, I get everyone in our house into the spirit by hanging mistletoe in a couple of doorways. Kissing beneath the mistletoe is an old custom that dates back to the Druids. The plant was believed to symbolize purity and strength and to bring happiness and peace and to promote romance. Enemies meeting beneath a sprig of mistletoe were said to become disarmed and kept their truce throughout the day.

Last of the ancient customs is our beautiful Christmas tree. The tree, always an evergreen, is regarded as a symbol of everlasting life. The lights that are put on a Christmas tree were originally meant to rekindle the sun's light and to bring the family warmth throughout the holiday season. Knowing these customs gives Christmas a special meaning to me and my family. As we decorate, we enjoy a feeling of peace and happiness and love.

A SAFE TREE

There are two choices when purchasing a Christmas tree—a live tree (my choice) or a cut tree. When choosing a cut tree, please keep these safety tips in mind to minimize the risk of fire.

A dry tree is a fire hazard. Before purchasing a cut tree, strike the butt against the ground sharply. A shower of needles means the tree has already dried out.

Before placing the tree in water, make a fresh cut at the base of the trunk to expose new wood for better water uptake.

Keep the container of your tree always full of water. A fresh tree can drink several gallons of water in the first few days in your home.

Never place a tree near a fireplace, radiator, television set, or other heat source. Keep the room cool to minimize drying.

Keep your tree fresh as long as possible and reduce fire hazard by spraying the entire tree thoroughly with an antidesiccant such as Safer's "ForEverGreen."

Check each set of lights, new or old, for broken or cracked sockets, frayed or bare wires, or loose connections. Discard any damaged lights or repair them before use.

Use no more than three standard-size sets of lights per single extension cord.

Never use lighted candles on or near a tree or other evergreens.

Don't burn Christmas greens in your fireplace.

Fantastica amaryllis and a laeliocattleya orchid make lavish decorations for a tablescape in the salon. This room is kept cool except when I have guests and there is a fire in the fireplace, so flowers like these last for several weeks.

RIGHT: *Here, dwarf myrtles, a small-leaved English ivy, and rosemary clipped into a wreath have holiday bows and are ready to decorate the house or to use as gifts.*

They throw sparks that could ignite whatever they land on.

Plan for safety. Always look for and eliminate what common sense tells you is a potential danger.

GIFT IDEAS FOR FRIENDS WHO GARDEN

Finding gifts for your gardening friends can be a lot of fun. The possibilities are practically endless, because there are so many fabulous gardening items on the market. Of course, during the holiday season, it may seem difficult to locate gardening products, since most garden centers and nurseries are stocked with holiday trimmings and Christmas trees. But most of these centers have the items, they're just not prominently displayed—so ask for what you want. And being so late in the season, you might even get the product at a reduction.

Consider a nursery gift certificate (redeemable in spring) for a shrub or tree. Gardening equipment is another possibility. Tools and equipment—such as an electric hedge trimmer, leaf blower, wheelbarrow, sprinkler, or nozzle—range from large to small and from expensive to moderately priced. I think a hose is one of the best gift items. Sometimes, I create gift baskets and tie on cheery bows.

Here are the essential tools for indoor gardeners:

hand-held fork for loosening the soil around potted plants, hand-held clippers, light trowel for transplanting, rubbing alcohol and cotton swabs to control mealybugs and brown scale, sponge for cleaning foliage, raffia for natural ties, and small bamboo stakes and plant markers and a marking pen for identifying plant varieties.

Small items make excellent stocking stuffers. Hand tools, such as pruners and clippers of all kinds, or a bulb planter, summer-flowering bulbs and pre-cooled bulbs, such as paper-whites and Chinese sacred lilies, are all nifty presents.

Indoor potted plants are another superb gift for avid gardeners. But, before choosing a plant for a gift, it is important to consider what will fit into the recipient's environment. In other words, don't buy a large plant for a person who has a tiny apartment or select a flowering one for someone who doesn't have a sunny window or a spot in which it can thrive.

Some of my favorite flowering plants for giving as gifts are Christmas cactus, calla lily, azalea, amaryllis, and streptocarpus. But, since not everyone has a green thumb, be sure to select a plant that will be easy and fun for beginners and individuals who profess to have no luck growing things. Philodendrons, snake plants, and asparagus ferns will flourish in almost any growing conditions. And, why not make your Christmas plants more festive by planting them in a basket or decorative container with a big, red holiday bow on top of them?

C. Z.'S SPECIAL HOLIDAY TODDY

Start with a big pot of apple cider, add three or four cinnamon sticks, and about a dozen cloves. Heat slowly. Don't boil. When it's steaming hot, ladle this mixture into a mug and add as much rum as you dare! Be sure not to get any loose cloves in the mug.

You can leave the spiced cider simmering on the stove all day, and the aroma that fills your kitchen is divine! So, any time you feel like a little taste of holiday cheer, just grab the ladle and the rum.

CHRISTMAS COLORS

My color choices for the Christmas dinner table are always red, white, and green—red candles, garlands of greenery, and bowls of paper-white narcissi, which have a fragrance that is out of this world.

For the week after Christmas, I like to keep the same festive colors throughout the house. The paper-white narcissi will last two weeks if they are kept in a cool place.

The poinsettia is a most popular plant for the Christmas holidays. The United States' first ambassador to Mexico, Joel Poinsett, came upon it in its native habitat of Mexico and introduced it back home. The bright red and sometimes white flowers, really bracts, have come to symbolize the holiday season for many. If given proper care, a poinsettia can bloom again the following year, and for years to come.

The requirements are not difficult. Proper watering is most important; water well as soon as the soil surface approaches being dry but never so much that the soil remains soggy for several days. Overwatering and drafts often cause leaf drop; remember, poinsettias are heat and humidity lovers. If you're lucky, your poinsettia could continue blooming until Easter. When the blooms fade, withhold water and place out of the light in a warm spot as the plant goes into dormancy. In early May, trim back the plant to two or three nodes (small swellings on the stem), start watering, and place in direct sunlight. When the frost is gone, just plunge your plant—pot and all—into the ground in a sunny spot outdoors in your garden. Fertilize occasionally and water during the hot months.

Now comes the important part. In September, when the nights get cool, bring in your poinsettia and try to maintain temperatures around 60 degrees F (15 degrees C), and give it fourteen hours of total darkness *every* night. Cover or closet it to be sure it gets no light from sundown to sunup until Thanksgiving. Any light at night during that period will interfere

Paper-white narcissi in the cool, bright bay window of the blue-and-white salon. Every week or so through October and early November, we start more narcissus bulbs so that the flowering season extends through New Year's.

Although poinsettias come in creamy white, pink, and bicolored forms, I prefer the old-fashioned red ones, displayed with the plastic growing pots slipped inside clay containers such as this one made from the imprint of very large cabbage leaves.

Scarlet amaryllis and paper-white
narcissi about to burst into bloom help
celebrate Christmas in the library.

RIGHT: *Holiday cactus decorate the*
library before Christmas.

with its cycle, and it won't bloom. During the day, give it full sun, but as soon as darkness falls, back to bed again. Come Christmas, your poinsettia should be full of buds.

Another traditional holiday plant is the Christmas cactus *(Schlumbergera bridgesii),* with drooping, red flowers. This species, along with the Thanksgiving cactus *(Schlumbergera truncata),* blooms with the shorter fall days and cool nights. A third species, called the Easter cactus *(Rhipsalidopsis gaertneri),* flowers in spring as the days grow longer. All of these glorious holiday plants can be propagated from leaf cuttings set to root in sandy soil mix in the spring. Thanksgiving and Christmas cactus—and more recently created hybrid cultivars in many colors, from white to palest pink to an orange that I favor, all known generally as holiday cactus—set buds when night temperatures fall regularly to below 55 degrees F (13 degrees C). They will bloom regardless of temperature if they have short days of nine hours and very long nights of fifteen hours, but for most of us it is easier to find a windowsill or other growing space where fall temperatures are just naturally cold enough at night to set the buds on holiday cactus.

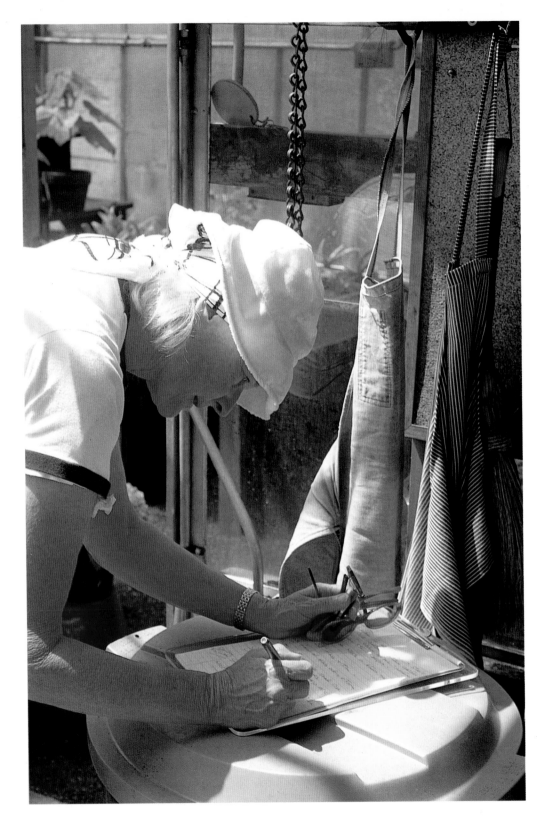

Here, I am organizing in the greenhouse, making lists of things that need doing for next year's garden.

HOLIDAYS FROM OFFICE PLANT CARE
AT HOLIDAY TIME

If you work in an office that closes for several days during the holidays and you have plants you love, there's no need to bring them all home with you. There's a simple solution. First, give them all a good drink of water; the water should come right through the drainage hole at the bottom of the pot. Then, group them together and cover them with tents made out of light plastic bags, such as those that come from the dry cleaners. This will help hold moisture. Be sure your grouping is in bright light but out of direct sun. When you get back after the holidays, immediately give your plants a good soaking, and they'll never know you've been away! (This same technique works well for plants at home—try placing them in a bathtub also.)

If your plants are too large to place under bags, plant services may be hired to care for office plants on a regular basis. Don't neglect your office plants— especially if you work in an office with nonopening windows or around smokers. Plants in these situations can be healthful as well as decorative. Vigorous leafing plants actually provide a source of oxygen. The pothos vine, or devil's ivy, is one of the best oxygen producers for an office, provided the vines receive ample light from nearby windows.

AFTER-HOLIDAY RENEWAL

When January arrives and the New Year's celebration is over, it is time to unwind with a feeling of fatigue and a little sadness. Time to put all the Christmas tree ornaments back in their boxes for another year.

I always get a live Christmas tree (the roots balled and covered), and immediately after the first of the year, I plant it in a predug hole. Of course, you're hearing this again: PLAN AHEAD! But with simple planning, you can have a great Christmas tree for the holidays and then a wonderful new tree for your property. Just be sure you dig the hole before the ground freezes, and fill it to one-third with mulch from your fall cleanup to keep the bottom from freezing.

It gives me great pleasure to be able to plant my tree after the holidays. As with everything in the garden, it means the continuous renewal of life. If you have no room or desire to plant more evergreens on your property, don't throw away that cut Christmas tree. You can still share with your feathered friends and hang some delicious goodies on it. Just place the tree in your yard in a protected spot where you can see it from a window, or what about on a patio or open porch? It's perfectly okay to leave your tree in the stand you used indoors. Just make sure it's braced against blowing winds. However, even if it does topple, the birds will still use it for shelter.

Birds love bread crumbs, peanut butter paté, suet, sunflower seeds, and of course, specially prepared wild bird feed mixes. If you have workshop space, it's fun and easy to make bird-feed containers that you can paint with bright colors. If you don't have a workshop and the necessary tools, use your ingenuity; make containers from household items such as plastic food containers or milk cartons. An excellent, simple container is a pinecone; the bigger the better! Hang it on the tree so that small pockets formed by the scales can be filled with seeds.

Of course, the greater the variety of food you put out, the greater variety of birds you'll attract! If you have any holly berries left over from your Christmas wreaths, put them out, too! Once the tree is loaded with food, it won't take long before song sparrows, nuthatches, finches, chickadees, and a host of other birds stop by for a snack.

After all traces of the holidays have been packed away, I putter around the greenhouse. Everything is resting; it is the quiet time. The seed catalogs arrive in the mail, and I start to get excited thinking and planning for my great new garden next spring. Soon, we will start sowing vegetable and flower seeds in flats.

The Spring Holidays

What flowers do you enjoy for Valentine's Day and Easter, both of which will occur before spring plantings come up? Planning ahead is crucial for springtime holidays. And fall is the time to begin thinking about them and planting exactly what you want. For Easter especially, I love fragrant white flowers, such as lilies, freesias, and hyacinths that have been set in pots in a cool place the previous autumn.

If St. Patrick's Day is important to you, try growing shamrock; it's easy and takes little time. White clover (*Trifolium repens*) is very popular, and it is believed by many that St. Patrick used this plant to symbolize the Trinity. Sow seeds in January, and you will produce a potted crop about three inches tall by St. Patrick's Day.

LEFT: *Fragrant white hyacinths are perfect for Easter. If the holiday comes late, there are often hyacinths blooming in the garden that can be dug, potted, and brought inside. Only one spike or pot will perfume a large room.*

RIGHT: *On Mother's Day, we cut azaleas from around Templeton and arrange them all around a grapevine and Spanish moss wreath hung on the front door. Each stem "sips" from a florist water pick concealed and secured within the wreath.*

For the Fourth of July, these orangeglow vines (Senecio confusus) —trained on a vertical pipe with a steering-wheel shape at the top to hold them in the air—are in full bloom. They look like floral fireworks set in large ceramic pots.

RIGHT: This August photograph of my rose terrace dining table suggests the harvest bounty at this season. The orange ball flowers are Scadoxus multiflorus, amaryllids from South Africa that are extremely easy to grow. Between them is a rare laeliocattleya orchid, and behind it is a tall vanda orchid. The perfect blossom in a small, green wine bottle is the world's favorite rose, Peace.

I just sprinkle a pinch of seeds onto ready-to-grow, sterile Pro-mix potting soil in a three-inch pot and cover them with a one-eighth-inch layer of milled sphagnum moss. They need sunshine, water, and warm temperatures to grow—not much else, except tender loving care.

On Mother's Day, I pull out all the stops and bring into the house all orchids that are blooming, not to mention pots of geraniums, mandevillas, flowering maples, azaleas, begonias—you name it. My son Alexander has made it something of a tradition to take me shopping for this holiday at my favorite local nursery. One year, he might treat me to some yews I want to fill out a new hedge; another, we might concentrate on more Rothschild azaleas for beds in front of the house.

Summertime

The summer holidays seem to take care of themselves. For the Memorial Day weekend, I fill my house with whatever is blooming in the garden. I love to fill vases with a mix of cut flowers, such as roses, peonies, lilies, and lilacs. For the Fourth of July, there will be red roses, blue delphiniums, and lots of snowy Shasta daisies.

After midsummer, I don't plan for any holiday decorations until Halloween. But remember, midsummer is the time to begin harvesting flowers for drying. (See chapter 3, "Summer," for information on drying flowers.) Dried flowers can be made into wonderful, one-of-a-kind decorations and gifts for any holiday. Consider making garlands, wreaths, potpourris, sachets, corsages, tussie-mussies, pressed flower notecards, or just create bouquets out of your dried flowers. And, if those late summer–early fall long weekends, such as Labor Day, are important to you, be sure to plant your flowers accordingly.

Remember the rules: plan ahead, organize, and have a system. And, most of all, have fun!

Tallyho!

This graceful statue was given by Henry Phipps to his daughter (my mother-in-law) in 1910. It was made in 1710 by Coyzevox, a famous French sculptor of the eighteenth century. Only three casts were made and the original is still at Versailles.

PHOTOGRAPHER'S NOTE

When *House Beautiful* magazine first sent me to interview C. Z. Guest, in 1976 on the occasion of the publication of her first book, *First Garden,* neither of us could have imagined that we were about to meet a person who was to become a lifelong gardening friend. Retrospectively, I can see also that C. Z., more than any other individual, has encouraged my work as a garden photographer.

Here, in the pages of C. Z. Guest's *5 Seasons of Gardening,* we have the unusual opportunity of watching one gardener's garden grow, through photography done by one photographer on a regular basis beginning in June 1976 and ending with the photograph of C. Z. planting paper-whites in October 1991, a period of just over fifteen years. Since the garden has grown more beautiful as it has aged, and I hope I have become a better photographer, the bulk of the photographs chosen for this book have been made since 1989. Early on, I used Pentax cameras and a variety of Kodachrome and Ektachrome transparency films. Currently, I am using Nikon cameras and lenses and mostly a professional film from Fuji called Velvia, which is fine-grained and super color-saturated.

While C. Z.'s paramount rule for success in gardening is to plan ahead, if I have one for photography, it is to use a tripod, or at least a monopod, to steady the camera and make possible a correct exposure under the existing lighting conditions.

The second rule is to keep taking pictures! "Elvin, have you got your camera? Do you have any film? You've got to take a picture of the garden!" Nicer or more cherished words this photographer hardly ever hears, except of course when C. Z. calls and says the topiaries have been missing me and need a trim or that a box of new plant treasures has arrived at Templeton and awaits me at the potting bench, where I'd rather be on Sunday than almost anywhere else on earth.

Elvin McDonald
New York City, October 17, 1991

FAVORITE SUPPLIERS

By Category

GENERAL
Wayside Gardens
Hodges, SC 29695

White Flower Farm
Litchfield, CT 29695

BULBS
Ralph Cook
914/796-3492 (Westchester County, NY)
407/798-5513 (Palm Beach County, FL)

CHRYSANTHEMUMS
King's Mums
P.O. Box 368
Clements, CA 95227

GREENHOUSES
Hobby Greenhouse Association
Glen Terrace
Bedford, MA 01730

National Greenhouse Manufacturers Association
6 Honey Bee Lane
P.O. Box 1350
Taylors, SC 29687

HOUSEPLANTS, HERBS, PERENNIALS
Logee's Greenhouses
141 North St.
Danielson, CT 06239

ORCHIDS
Alberts & Merkel Bros., Inc.

2210 S. Federal Highway
Boynton Beach, FL 33435

Jones and Scully, Inc.
2200 Northwest 33rd Ave.
Miami, FL 33435

ROSES
Jackson & Perkins
P.O. Box 1028
Medford, OR 97501

SEEDS (FLOWER, FRUIT, AND VEGETABLE)
W. Atlee Burpee Seed Company
300 Park Ave.
Warminster, PA 18991

The Cook's Garden
P.O. Box 535
Londonderry, VT 05148

Gurney's Seed & Nursery Co.
Yankton, SD 57079

Geo. W. Park Seed Co., Inc.
Greenwood, SC 29647

Ronniger's Seed Potatoes
Star Route
Moyie Spring, ID 83845

TRELLIS DESIGN
William C. Mulligan
225 E. 57th St.
New York, NY 10022

INDEX

propagation, 34, 36–37
selection, 30, 32
toxicity of, 38
vacation care, 163
Houssaye, Roger, 8
Hoya. See Waxplant
Humidity and houseplants, 32
Hyacinth, 130, *164*
Hydrangea, 38, *39, 82–83, 86*

Impatiens, 36, 117
Indirect-light houseplants, 32
Indoor gardening, 118, 144. *See also* Houseplants
Insecticidal soap spray, 103, 118
Insects, 85, 88, 91, 140
Interplanting, 17
Iris, 57, 135
Iris, Dutch, 130
Iris, Siberian, *134*
Iris reticulata, 130
Ivy, 32
Ivy, English, *77, 119, 157, 161*
Ivy, German *(Senecio),* 32
Ivy, grape *(Cissus rhombifolia),* 30, 32
Ixora coccinea. See Flame-of-the-woods

Jack-o'-lanterns, 147
Jade plant *(Crassula argentea),* 32
Japanese beetles, *102,* 104
Jasmine, 32, *33,* 41
Jekyll, Gertrude, 119

Kalanchoe, 32, 36, 41, 147–148, *150*
Kitchen gardens, 13, *94, 132*
Kochia. See Summer cypress
Kohlrabi, 17

Labeling beds, 25, *52,* 53
Labor Day, gardening for, 168
Lady's slipper *(Paphiopedilum),* 75
Lantana, 32, 41, *115*
Larkspur, 54, 100
Laurel, mountain, 44
Lavandula dentata. See Lavender
Lavender *(Lavandula dentata),* 73, 96
Leadwort *(Pulmonaria),* 57
Leaf mulch, 140
Leaf spots, 38
Leek, *90*
Lemon-verbena *(Aloysia triphylla),* 73

Lettuce, 17
Lilium. See Lily
Lily, Asiatic hybrid, *82–83, 86*
Lily, calla, *24,* 130
Lily, Chinese trumpet, *84*
Lily *(Lilium),* 71, 130, 135
Lily of the valley, 130, 150
Lime, garden, 91, 140, 143
Linden trees, *131*
Lipstick vine *(Aeschynanthus),* 32
Livistona. See Chinese fan palm
Lizards, 88, *89,* 91
Low-light houseplants, 30
Lupine, 57, 135
Lutyens, Sir Edwin, 119

Mail-order seeds, 21, 23
Mandevilla sanderi. See Red Riding Hood
Mannoni, Marie, 8
Manure tea, 118
Maple, Japanese cutleaf, *116*
Marigold, 17, *18, 87,* 96, 100, 117
Marigold, marsh *(Caltha),* 57
McDonald, Elvin, 120
Mealybugs, 36
Melampodium, 96
Mellon, Bunny, 8
Melons, 113
Memorial Day, gardening for, 168
Mexican tuberose, 148, *151*
Microwave method of drying flowers, 100
Mildew, 91, 103
Milles, James, *74*
Miracid 30-10-10, 116
Mistletoe, 155
Mitriostigma. See African gardenia
Moluccella. See Bells of Ireland
Monarda. See Bee balm
Monkshood, 57
Morning glory, 96
Mosaic plant *(Fittonia),* 30
Moss, 117–118
Mother's Day, gardening for, 167
Moulin des Tuilleries, 121
Mountain laurel. *See* Laurel, mountain
Mowers, care of, 140, 143
Mulch, 43, 51, 53, *60,* 92, 95, 140, 143
Mulligan, William C., 132
Myrtle, dwarf, *157, 161*

Narcissus, 130
Nasturtium, 17, 117
Nicotiana, 96
Nitrogen in soil, 47
Norfolk Island pine *(Araucaria),* 32

Office environment plants, 32, 163
Okra, 100
Onions, 17
Orangeglow vine *(Senecio confusus),* 166
Orchid, 32, *36,* 77
Orchid, cattleya, *75, 79, 80, 144–145*
Orchid, dendrobium, *78, 80*
Orchid, laeliocattleya, *156, 167*
Orchid, vanda, *33, 144–145, 167*
Osmanthus fragrans. See Sweet olive
Osmocote (fertilizer), 36
Overhead sprinkling system, 92, *93*
Overwatering, 37
Oxalis regnellii. See Clover plant

Page, Russell, 120, 121–122
Paley, Babe, 8
Palms, 32
Pansy, 117
Paper-white narcissi, *129,* 150, *152, 159, 160*
Paphioperilum. See Lady's slipper
Parsley, 29
Pascucci, Mary, 8
Passiflora. See Passionflower
Passionflower *(Passiflora),* 32, *114*
Pasteurizing soil, 85
Patio gardening, 113, 117–118
Peas, 17
Peony, 57, 61, *81,* 130, 135–136
Peony, herbaceous, *134*
Peony, tree, *60,* 63
Peppers, 17, *128*
Peppers, ornamental, 96
Peppers, purple, *106*
Perennials
cultivation, 57–58, 61, 133, 135
hardiness of, 18
mulching, 43
propagation, 58
Periwinkle, 96
Perlargonium. See Geranium
Perovskia atriplicifolia. See Russian sage
Persian violet *(Exacum),* 41
Petunia, *54,* 117

Designed by Martine Bruel
Set in Garamond Light and Book (ITC) by Hamilton Phototype
Printed and bound by Tien Wah Press Ltd., Singapore